Swatch Critters
FROM THE PIN LOOM

Step-by-Step Instructions
for Making 30 Cuddly Animals
from Woven Squares

Deb Essen

SCHIFFER
CRAFT

Other Schiffer Craft Books by the Author:
Easy Weaving with Supplemental Warps: Overshot, Velvet, Shibori, and More, ISBN 978-0-7643-6470-9
Profile Drafting for Handweavers: Designs, Projects & Expert Tips for Turning Your Ideas into Weave Structures, ISBN 978-0-7643-7000-7

Copyright © 2025 by Deb Essen

Library of Congress Control Number: 2024932368

Zoom LoomTM is a registered trademark of Schacht Spindle Company, Inc.

All rights reserved. No part of this work may be reproduced or used in any form or by any means—graphic, electronic, or mechanical, including photocopying or information storage and retrieval systems—without written permission from the publisher.

The scanning, uploading, and distribution of this book or any part thereof via the Internet or any other means without the permission of the publisher is illegal and punishable by law. Please purchase only authorized editions and do not participate in or encourage the electronic piracy of copyrighted materials.

"Schiffer Craft" and the crane logo are registered trademarks of Schiffer Publishing, Ltd.

Designed by Lori Malkin Ehrlich
Cover design by Lindsay Hess
Photo Stylist: Lori Wenger
Photographer (projects): Jason Masters
Type set in Calder LC & Dark/Omnes Regular & SemiBold

ISBN: 978-0-7643-6810-3
Printed in China

Published by Schiffer Craft
An imprint of Schiffer Publishing, Ltd.
4880 Lower Valley Road
Atglen, PA 19310
Phone: (610) 593-1777; Fax: (610) 593-2002
Email: Info@schifferbooks.com
Web: www.schifferbooks.com

For our complete selection of fine books on this and related subjects, please visit our website at www.schifferbooks.com. You may also write for a free catalog.

Schiffer Publishing's titles are available at special discounts for bulk purchases for sales promotions or premiums. Special editions, including personalized covers, corporate imprints, and excerpts, can be created in large quantities for special needs. For more information, contact the publisher.

We are always looking for people to write books on new and related subjects. If you have an idea for a book, please contact us at proposals@schifferbooks.com.

Dedication

For my mom who always
supported my creative side

Contents

INTRODUCTION:	The Swatch Critters Story	6
CHAPTER ONE:	Warp and Weave on Your Pin Loom	8
CHAPTER TWO:	Before You Begin	14
SPECIAL SECTION:	Creating Shapes for Multiple Critters	18
CHAPTER THREE:	The Projects	23

1 • Twodot the Turtle • 24

5 • Alzada the Angora Goat • 40

8 • Delphia the Fiber Fairy • 52

12 • Laurel the Lion • 68

2 • Pryor the Panda • 28

9 • Marias the Mermaid • 56

3 • Shelby and Sidney the Sheep • 32

6 • Libby the Llama • 44

13 • Frazer the Frog • 72

10 • Polaris the Penguin • 60

14 • Dagmar the Dragon • 76

4 • Harrison the Hedgehog • 36

7 • Eureka the Unicorn • 48

11 • Olney the Owl • 64

15 • Kiowa the Kangaroo • 80

19 • Hobson the Hippo • 98

23 • Ovando the Octopus • 120

27 • Bridger the Bison • 138

16 • Tarkio the T-Rex • 84

24 • Pablo the Peacock • 124

20 • Geraldine the Giraffe • 102

28 • Teton the Teddy Bear • 142

17 • Clancy the Chameleon • 90

25 • Forsyth the Fox • 128

21 • Rosebud the Rabbit • 108

29 • Darby the Dog • 148

18 • Ekalaka the Elephant • 94

26 • Gardiner the Grizzly Bear • 134

22 • Cascade the Cat • 114

30 • Kinsey the Kitty • 154

Appendix 162
    Face Patterns 162
    Weaving with a Different-Colored Yarn 163
    How to Weave Twill Squares 164
    Weaving Patterns 166

Acknowledgments 168

INTRODUCTION

The Swatch Critters Story

IT ALL STARTED IN 2013. I was at the National Needlearts Association's summer wholesale trade show. This event is where yarn shops go to shop, and I was there to sell weaving kits for my business, dje handwovens.

2013 was also the year that Schacht Spindle Company introduced the Zoom Loom™, their reinvention of 4-inch pin looms in collaboration with John Mullarkey. Jane Patrick, one of the owners, approached me with a Zoom Loom in hand and asked if I'd be interested in creating kits using the squares woven on the Zoom Loom. I immediately said, "Yes!"

Pin looms appeared on the weaving scene in the 1930s as small wooden frames with nails around the perimeter that hold yarn to allow the weaving of small squares. The best-known brand was the "Weaveit" pin loom. Now I have to admit, previous experience with pin looms made out of wood did not make me a fan of pin loom weaving. The wooden looms can be hard to hold comfortably, the weaving needle would catch on the frame edges, and the nails are not always perfectly spaced.

But Schacht Spindle Company's Zoom Loom resolved all the issues I had with pin looms. The frame is flat plastic that is easy to hold, the pins are placed precisely and securely anchored, the inside edges of the frame are beveled so the weaving needle does not catch a sharp edge when exiting, and as a bonus, the loom frame has directional notations for winding yarn onto the pin loom. I am in love with these little looms!

At the time, several of my weaving kits used yarn from a small company specializing in hand-painted knitting yarns located in our mountain valley in Montana. When I got home from the trade show, I grabbed some Mountain Colors yarn and wove some practice squares. Turns out pin looms and knitting yarns play together really well.

I contemplated what kind of project kit I could create with these little squares—a scarf was obvious but felt rather uninspired. A pillow cover? A shawl? As I was weaving with some green yarn, I thought, "I wonder if I can make a turtle?" My first attempt looked more like an armadillo, but in the end, yes, I created a turtle! I brought him to Mountain Colors to get their opinions and received enthusiastic "thumbs up" all around. Eileen, their office manager, coined the perfect name: a "Swatch Critter." Over the next ten years I created Critters of all shapes and sizes and sold kits to yarn shops across the country so fiber enthusiasts could create their own Swatch Critters.

All the Swatch Critters were named for locations in Montana. Many of the towns I named Critters for are technically "unincorporated towns," which means the towns do not have a local government of mayor, town council, police, et al. but are regulated under the county the town is located in. Montana has many unincorporated towns, most are very small, but some are growing but still keeping their unincorporated status.

Eventually I retired the kits, but the Swatch Critters with their fun personalities stayed as popular as ever, and weavers continued to ask me if patterns were available. The result is the pattern book in your hands, featuring all the Swatch Critters I created. I hope you enjoy making them for many years to come.

Happy creating!

Deb Essen

CHAPTER ONE

Warp and Weave on Your Pin Loom

FOR THOSE OF YOU who have never woven on a pin loom (or it's been awhile and you need a review), this chapter is for you! I use a Zoom Loom™ pin loom, so most of the references are based on it. But the warping / weaving instructions also apply to most pin looms. (I say "most" because there may be slight differences in pin placement / spacing on various styles of pin looms.) The Zoom Loom™ is easy to hold and has markings on the frame at the corners to help navigate as you weave.

> **All the Critters are made from 4-inch pin loom squares. No squares are cut in the making of the Critters. Calculate 8 yards of yarn per 4-inch woven square.**

If you don't have a Zoom Loom™, you will find it handy to mark the corners of your loom with the following reference numbers, using a felt-tipped pen:

  lower left corner: 1,
  lower right corner: 2,
  upper left corner: 3, and
  upper right corner: 4.

Winding the Yarn onto the Loom

Use your dominant hand to wind the yarn onto the loom and to weave. Since a majority of humans are right-handed, the following instructions are written for the right-handed weaver. But with a couple of simple adjustments, left-handed weavers can follow the same instructions.

For right-handed weavers: To begin winding your yarn on the loom, position the loom so the starting point / slot in the outside edge marked with a "1" on the frame is at the *lower left*. I like to lay my loom on my lap when I wind the yarn onto the loom. You may find it easier to lay the loom on a table.

For left-handed weavers: Position the loom so the starting point / slot corner labeled "1" is at the *upper right* so it's easier to work with your dominant hand. The number notations on the frame will still

pertain in the following instructions as you wind the yarn onto the pin loom. However, references of up vs. down will be reversed. Example: If the instructions say, "Bring the yarn straight up to the top of the loom . . . " you will actually be bringing the yarn straight down to what is still technically the top edge of the loom.

Tip for left-handed weavers: It may help to turn this book upside down when referring to the winding photos because then the photo will match what your loom looks like in front of you.

Winding the Warp onto the Loom

Tuck the end of your yarn into the slot on the frame, leaving about a 3-to-4-inch tail. If your pin loom does not have a slot, a little piece of the hooked surface of hook-and-loop fastener tape attached to the outside edge or underside of the loom works well to hold the yarn tail. Place the yarn in the opening between vertical and horizontal pins. Bring the yarn straight up right next to the vertical row of pins to the top edge of the loom, exiting in the small opening at the corner marked "3." This is the start of Round #1.

Left-handers: Bring the yarn straight down to the bottom edge of the loom, right next to the pins.

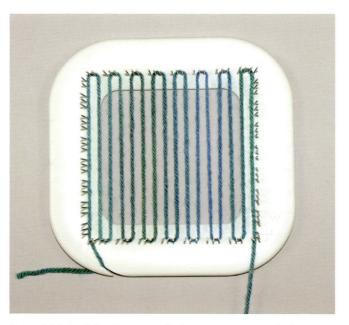

Round 1: Wind the first round of yarn onto your pin loom.

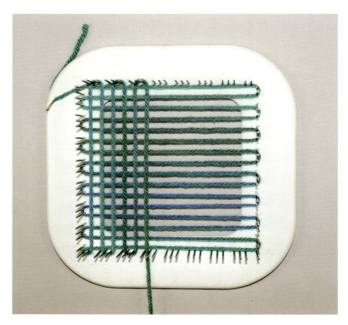

Round 2: Turn the loom 90 degrees to the right. Wind Round 2 on your pin loom—note the small loop at the lower corner that goes around two pins.

Round #1: Bring the yarn around the first 2 pins on the right at the top, then bring the yarn back to the bottom so that there are 2 pins to the left of the yarn and 2 pins to the right of the yarn. Bring the yarn around the 2 pins on the right and bring yarn back up to the top, placing the yarn in the large space, with one pin to the left and 2 pins to the right of the yarn. Wrap around the 2 pins on the right and then back down. Continue winding in this pattern until you reach the lower right-hand corner of the loom and your yarn comes out *between* the bottom 2 pins by the corner marked number "2" on the loom frame. IMPORTANT! *Your yarn should be taut but not stretched tight across the loom.*

Tip: As I'm winding the yarn on the loom, after I've gone around 2 pins, I like to place a fingertip from my nondominant hand on the yarn loop around the outside edge of the 2 pins I've just gone around. I hold it there just long enough for the yarn to reach the opposite side, then after going around the new pins, fingertip touch, pull yarn across, etc. This helps prevent accidently popping the yarn off the pins as I wind. Think of your fingertip as a very temporary yarn stopper.

Round #2: Rotate the entire loom a quarter turn to the right so the starting tail at the #1 corner is now at the upper left and your winding yarn is at the lower left-hand #2 corner of the loom. Bring the yarn around the first 2 vertical pins that are right next to each other on the lower left, and bring the yarn into the large opening between the sets of pins. There will be 2 pins right next to each other on the left, with the yarn wrapped around both pins and three pins close together to the right of the yarn. Bring the yarn straight across the loom. On this side, there will be one pin to the left of the yarn and 2 pins to the right of the yarn. Bring the yarn around the 2 pins on the right, then straight across the loom, and wrap the yarn around 2 pins on the right. Continue winding this round until you reach the upper right-hand corner labeled #3 and the yarn exits between the 2 pins at that corner.

WARP AND WEAVE ON YOUR PIN LOOM

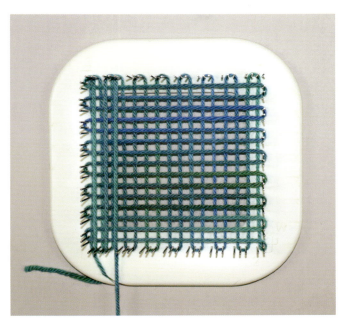

Round 3: Wind Round 3 on your pin loom—note the small loops around the pins at opposite corners: One loop by the "2" notation on the frame and the second on the opposite corner by the "3."

Round #3: Turn the loom a quarter turn to the left, so the warp yarn is at the upper left corner now. Bring the yarn around the 2 corner pins, 1 on each side of the corner, following the arrow at that corner of the loom. This round of yarn will lie between the yarns wound in Round 1 and will again go around 2 pins at each edge, with 1 pin between each row. Continue winding until you get to the lower right-hand corner.

Measuring the Weft

Without cutting the yarn, wind the yarn counterclockwise (clockwise if you are left-handed) around the outside of all the pins for 5 rounds, stopping just past the lower left-hand #1 corner on the frame where you started warping the loom. This is the weft / weaving yarn you will use to weave the square. Cut the weft yarn.

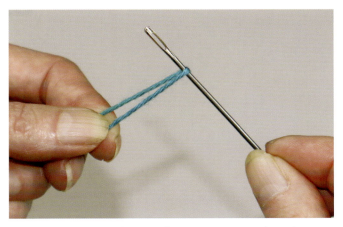

Threading the weaving needle, step 1: It's much easier to thread your needle if you first fold the yarn over the needle.

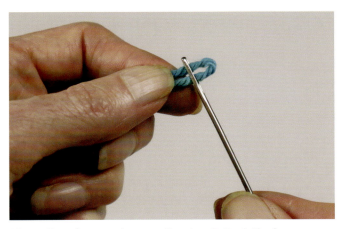

Threading the weaving needle, step 2: Push the loop through the eye of the needle, grab the loop, and pull the end of the yarn through.

There are two needles with your pin loom. The long needle is the weaving needle. The shorter needle is the yarn needle used to stitch together your Critter. Thread the cut end of the weft / weaving yarn onto the long weaving needle. It's easier to thread the needles if you fold the yarn over the needle to create a small, tight loop and push the loop through the eye of the needle.

Weaving

Once you have the yarn on the loom, weaving is much easier if you hold the loom in your non-dominant hand. As you weave the first row, it's easy to accidently pop the loops off the pins. If one loop pops off, you can slip it back onto the pins. If multiple loops pop off at the same time, it's easier to remove the needle and rewind the yarn onto the loom. Trust me. I've been there.

It's not cheating to place a finger or edge of the thumb of your nondominant hand against the yarn loops that are around the pins when weaving the first row. In fact, I recommend it. Once that first row of weaving is done, the yarns are anchored, and you are off to the races.

Tip: When weaving, hold the yarn end of the weaving needle and gently rock the tip of the needle (don't lift the entire needle) over / under the yarns across the row to help prevent popping the square off the loom prematurely.

If you are right-handed: Hold the loom so the slot / corner 1 of the frame is in the lower left corner. You will begin weaving at the lower right corner of the loom, marked with the #2 on the frame. There is a small loop around the 2 pins in that corner. The tip of your weaving needle goes over the outside loop that is around the pins and then immediately goes under the other side of the loop, which is the next thread in line. Continue over / under across the loom.

If you are left-handed: Hold the pin loom so the corner marked #1 is at the upper right and the corner of the loom marked #2 is at the upper left as you look at the loom. You will also begin weaving at the corner marked #2. Insert the tip of the weaving needle over the outside of the corner loop and immediately under the next yarn, which is the second part of that small loop.

Whether you are right- or left-handed, after you complete a pick (row) of weaving, pull the weft yarn through so the yarn is snug against the pins where you started. Turn the loom 180 degrees so you can use your dominant hand to weave across, always starting over a loop.

Tip: Note that around the loom, yarn loops go around the back of two pins, followed by a space without a loop and with a single pin. *You will always start weaving OVER a loop at the side of the loom and exit where there isn't a loop on the opposite side.*

Note the really small loop around the 2 pins at the lower right corner. When you begin weaving, your needle tip goes over the outside of the loop and then under the next thread that is the other side of this loop. Then continue over/under across the loom. You will do the same with the small loop around 2 pins in the upper left-hand corner, by the "3" on the loom. Note that the rows of yarn on the loom now alternate between a higher position (Round 3) and lower position (Round 1). You weave over the higher-position yarns and under the lower-position yarns.

WARP AND WEAVE ON YOUR PIN LOOM

You will always enter your needle into a row over the loop that goes around the outside of the pins, then under the first yarn on the loom and over the next yarn. Continue over / under and exit on the opposite side where there is not a loop around the pins after weaving across.

The last row of weaving enters over the small loop around the corner pins and then immediately goes under the next yarn, and your needle will be right next to the pins. Make sure you get this last row of weaving completed so your square is stable on all edges.

Tip: Note that the third round of yarn you wound on the loom sits higher than the first round of yarn. As you weave across, you will always weave OVER the threads that are UP (push down the yarn with the tip of the weaving needle) and weave UNDER threads that are DOWN in a row.

Tip: When you are ready to start the next pick (row) of weaving, you will find you have a row of yarn between the pick you just wove and the next pick you are starting. These yarns were placed on the loom in Round 2 and are what I call a "freebie" pick. Because of the way the yarn is wound on the loom, the freebie pick will be automatically woven between the picks you weave with your needle. Freebie picks have a tendency to infringe upon the space where you need to weave next. Simply take the point of your weaving needle and push that freebie pick toward the pick(s) already woven to make a little space where you are going to weave another pick of yarn. The freebie picks mean that after weaving across 2 times, you will actually have 3 rows woven.

Weaving the last row: Your last row of weaving will be right against the pins and starts at the corner with "3" on the frame. Just like when you started, you go over the first thread that is around the pins and immediately go under the next yarn, which is actually from the first round, then over the other side of the loop. It's a tight space. Make sure you get that last row woven or you won't have a nice tight square.

Weaving in the yarn tails: After completing your last row of weaving, place the tip of the weaving needle between the last and next-to-last woven rows and weave three or four picks back into the square. Pull your yarn through and cut the yarn close to the fabric. This weaves in your tail of yarn and leaves a tidy square. Thread the starting tail onto the shorter yarn needle and weave that end back into the fabric three or four picks. Pull the tail through and trim close to the fabric. Pop the square off the loom!

CHAPTER TWO
Before You Begin

#1: Select your pin loom. All Critters are based on 4-inch pin loom squares woven out of knitting yarn, using any pin loom that weaves 4-inch squares. You do *not* need several different sizes or shapes of pin looms to make the Critters!

#2: Select your yarn. Recommended yarn weights for weaving squares are: DK or light worsted weight knitting yarns in wool, wool blends, superwash wool, acrylic, or cotton. You will need 8 yards of yarn per woven square. The amounts of yarn you need for each project are listed under "Supplies Needed." Handspun or commercial yarns both work great!

#3: Check the sett on your pin loom. The Zoom Loom™ weaves at eight ends per inch for sett. This is the perfect sett for squares out of DK or light worsted knitting yarns. To check the size of a yarn, wrap the yarn around a ruler for 1 inch (do not stretch the yarn while wrapping or squish wraps tightly together or leave space between the wraps). Count the number of wraps of yarn in 1 inch. Yarns of the best size will be 12–16 wraps per inch. For weaving sett calculation, divide the number of wraps by 2 (because there is both warp and weft in a woven inch). Yes, these yarns are technically a sett of six to eight ends per inch. Yes, you can use smaller-gauge yarns, but if the space between the woven yarns is too large, your stuffing will show (and maybe even come out!). Yes, you can use finer yarns by doubling the yarn so you are winding / weaving with two lengths of yarn at the same time.

#4: With any new yarn, weave a test square first! This is the time to test that the yarn you've selected will create a nice stable square that will hold its shape when you make the different parts of the Critters. Too large a yarn and you may not be able to weave an entire square or the fabric may be too dense to fold nicely into the various shapes. Too fine a yarn, and the spaces between the yarn intersections will allow the stuffing to escape / show. Wash the test square and lay flat to dry before passing final judgment.

#5: Weave all squares with a 3-to-4-inch beginning tail. This is done so that you can weave the tail back into the square over / under three or four threads between the first and second rows of weaving, using the yarn needle before you take the square off the loom. When you finish the square, use the weaving needle to weave that yarn end back into the square. Trim both tails close to the fabric. Then remove the square from the loom.

BEFORE YOU BEGIN

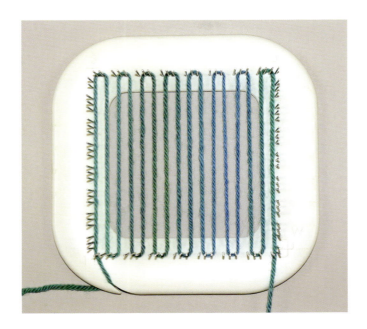

#6: When you wind the yarn onto the loom, keep moderate tension on the yarn. But the tension shouldn't be super tight, or it will be very hard to weave. The yarn should be taut, not tight, and also not sag for most yarns. The exception is 100% cotton yarns. These yarns have less elasticity than wool or acrylic knitting yarns, so cotton needs be wound onto the loom very loosely. As you weave, that looseness will be taken up by the interlacement of the yarns. Weave that test square!

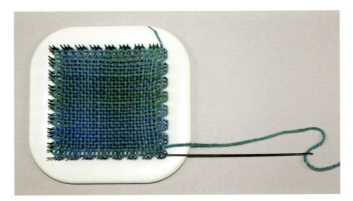

IMPORTANT TIP! *When you are weaving your squares, your weaving needle will ALWAYS enter OVER a loop around the side pins of the loom. This is how you know you are starting a row of weaving in the correct spot.*

#7: Hand-wash all squares in warm soapy water. Rinse, gently squeeze out water, and lay flat to dry before sewing them together. This will remove any spinning oils from the yarns plus block your squares into shape, and any space between the threads will close up. Off the loom and after washing, the yarns will move closer together as they travel over and under each other (filling the holes) and the squares shrink a little in size. This is to be expected. The squares will measure about 3½–3¾ inches square after washing and drying.

#8: Review the project instructions. They refer to right and wrong sides of the fabric when sewing the squares together. The wrong side is where you see the seam edges. The right side is where you see the seam lines only.

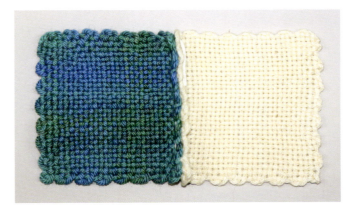

Seam edges show = WRONG side of fabric

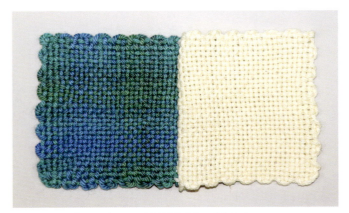

Only seam lines show = RIGHT side of fabric

15

#9: Practice hand stitching. If you can sew a button or a hem, you can make a Swatch Critter.

Running stitch

#10: Use the same yarn as the squares for stitching squares together. All seams are ¼-inch seams (stitch between first and second weaving rows) unless noted otherwise in the instructions. Use a running stitch with a stitch length no longer than ¼ inch. **Note:** Many of the how-to photos in the book use a contrasting stitching yarn so you can see the stitching lines in the photo.

Whip stitch through the loops

Slip stitch

BEFORE YOU BEGIN

#11: Review the stitching instructions. Exceptions to ¼-inch seams are noted in the instructions in the patterns. Some instructions call for whip stitching seams through the loops on the edges of the squares. Slip stitch is used to close openings after stuffing or attaching various body parts.

#12: Pay attention to the orders of the Critters. Patterns progress from the easiest Critters to assemble to Critters with more complicated assembly instructions. Many of the body shapes are repeated in different Critters, so you will find familiar instructions in many patterns. I have created a special section with step-by-step photos for the techniques used for the repeated body shapes in the various Critters.

> All the Swatch Critters are named for locations in their home state of Montana!

SPECIAL SECTION

Creating Shapes for Multiple Critters

AS I CREATED MORE CRITTERS, I discovered that many of the shapes created from squares could be used in multiple Critters. This section has step-by-step photos and instructions for these repeated shapes. It's a one-stop reference.

Return here to find how to create a new shape from a square. Be sure to follow the specific directions for seaming / stitching in some of the shapes as noted in the individual patterns.

Rounded Body: Turtle, Panda, Teddy Bear, Big Kitty

STEP 1: Take 2 squares and place them on top of each other, matching the edges and corners. Stitch a ¼-inch seam on one edge. Open into rectangle two squares long. Repeat with another 2 squares. Place the 2 rectangles on top of each other, with right sides together. Stitch a ¼-inch seam along one long edge. Open. You have a large square consisting of 4 squares. Set large square aside and repeat to create a second large square.

STEP 2: Lay the first large square on a flat surface, with the right side up. Lay the second large square on top so right sides are together and the points of the top square are lined up with the seam lines of the bottom square.

STEP 3: Pin the points of the top square to the seam lines of the bottom square.

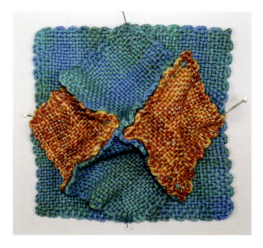

18

CREATING SHAPES FOR MULTIPLE CRITTERS

STEP 4: Pin the points of the bottom square to the seam lines of the top square. Match and pin the remaining edges between the pinned points of the squares. Stitch a ¼-inch seam all the way around the edges, leaving a small opening in the seam to turn the body right side out.

STEP 5: Turn body right side out and stuff to desired firmness and shape. Slip stitch the seam opening closed. One side of the body will have the seam lines running straight across the body. The other side will have the seam lines on the diagonal. Which Critter you are making will determine which side of the body you will use as the front vs. the back.

Basic Legs: Turtle, Panda, Rabbit, Dragon, Kangaroo, Grizzly Bear, Kitty, Fox

STEP 1: Fold a square in half, matching the edges. Stitch a ¼-inch seam along the long edge and one short edge. Turn right side out through the end opening.

STEP 2: The narrow-seamed end is the "foot" end of the leg. If you want a shorter leg (for example, the turtle), fold the open end of the leg to the inside of the leg until you achieve the desired length for the leg. Stuff the leg to desired firmness.

STEP 3: To add a "foot," after stuffing, pinch the seamed end of the leg to create a foot of desired size, making sure the seam lines are at the back of the leg / bottom of the foot. Either slip stitch the edges of the fold together (panda feet / legs) or stitch a tack stitch (repeated running stitch) through all layers of the leg (dragon and kangaroo).

19

Small Closed Tube: Bodies of Sheep, Goat, Llama, Unicorn, Hippo, Lion's Body, Peacock's Body, Dog's Head

STEP 1: Take two squares and lay them on top of each other, matching the edges and corners. Stitch a ¼-inch seam on two opposite edges. You have a small tube open on each end. Leave tube with wrong side out.

STEP 2: Take another square and place it into one open end of the tube, matching opposite points to the seam lines on each side of the tube. The points should be about ½ inch above the edge of the tube edge. Now pin the 2 remaining points to the edge of the opening, halfway between the tube's seam lines.

Pin the points to the tube opening, with the points about ½ inch above the edge of the tube. Stitch a ¼-inch seam around the square / tube opening, rounding the seam past the points. Repeat for the other end of the tube but leave a small opening in this seam to turn the tube right side out.

STEP 3: Stuff the closed tube to the desired firmness and shape so the ends bulge out a bit for chest and bum. Slip stitch the seam opening closed.

CREATING SHAPES FOR MULTIPLE CRITTERS

Neck Shape: Goat, Llama, Unicorn, Owl's Wings, Grizzly, Dog

STEP 1: Fold down 1 point on a square so it measures 1 inch from the point to the fold.

STEP 2: With the folded point on the outside, fold in half so the points match. Stitch a ¼-inch seam from folded-back point edge to the matched points. Turn right side out so the folded-under point is inside the neck. The end with the folded-back point is the head end of the neck. The larger opening will be placed on the "chest" end of the body.

Cone: Legs for Llama, Unicorn, Frog, Octopus, Elephant, and Bison. Feathers for the Peacock. Wings and arms for the Fiber Fairy. Neck for Dragon and Kangaroo. Tail tips for T-Rex and Chameleon. *(This is a very versatile shape!)*

STEP 1: Fold a square into triangle shape by matching points diagonally across from each other in a square. Whip stitch through the loops (or stitch a ¼-inch seam, depending on the Critter pattern instructions) on one edge from the fold to the center point. Leave the other edge from the center point to the fold open.

STEP 2: Center the seam line below the open point to make a "kite" shape. Follow the directions for individual Critters for closing the opening.

Large Tube: Body for Hedgehog, Penguin, Owl, Fox, Kinsey the Kitty, Darby the Dog

THIS BASIC CLOSED TUBE is used for the bodies of the hedgehog, penguin, owl, lion, and fox. It is also used for Teton the Teddy, Kinsey the Kitty, and Darby the Dog's legs and body. Follow the instructions in each Critter instructions for the number of squares used for the tube shape.

STEP 1: In the color order specified in the individual Critter's pattern, take 2 squares and lay them on top of each other, matching edges and points. Stitch a ¼-inch seam along one edge. Open. Place a third square on top of one of the joined squares, matching edges. Stitch a ¼-inch seam on the outside edge parallel to the first seam. You now have a rectangle 3 squares long.

Repeat to make another 3-square rectangle. Place the 2 rectangles on top of each other, matching long edges. Stitch a ¼-inch seam along one long edge only. Open. You have a larger rectangle 2 squares high by 3 squares long.

STEP 2: Fold the rectangle in half the long way so the 2 square ends match with right sides together. Stitch a ¼-inch seam across the 2-square end. You now have a tube that is three squares around and 2 squares high. Do not turn the tube yet.

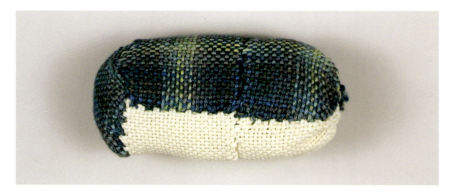

STEP 3: Closing the ends. The seam lines should be on the outside of the tube. Take another square and place it into 1 end of the tube so 1 point matches the center back seam line of the tube and the opposite point is centered on the opposite square. Pin both points so the points are even with the edge of the tube. Pin remaining points to the sides of the tube halfway between the pinned points. Stitch a ¼-inch seam around the opening, easing extra fabric as necessary. Depending on the Critter, you will either insert another square in the other open end or move to Step 4.

STEP 4: Turn the body tube right side out and stuff to desired shape / firmness. Stitch a gathering (running) stitch around the opening about ¼ inch away from the edge. Pull the ends of the gathering stitch yarn and pull tight like a drawstring bag. Tie the ends of the gathering stitch yarn together.

THE PROJECTS

PROJECT 1
Twodot the Turtle

THE PROJECTS

TWODOT THE TURTLE is the Critter that started it all, so it's appropriate that Twodot is the first project in the book. Plus, Twodot is one of the easiest Critters to assemble, and many of the pattern's body shapes are repeated in other Critters. Twodot the Turtle is named for the census-designated town of Twodot in Wheatland County in central Montana. Yes, the place really exists. Yes, it's a really small town, population 26 souls. Yes, depending on whom you ask, that's how it's spelled, although technically the US Postal Service changed it to Two Dot in 1999. The town was named for the cattle brand consisting of two dots of rancher George R. Wilson, the man who originally donated the land to establish the town back in 1900.

Supplies Needed

88 yards green DK or light worsted knitting yarn
16 yards orange DK or light worsted knitting yarn
2 yards black fingering weight yarn or embroidery floss for face
Stuffing of your choice

Weave the squares as follows:

11 squares of green yarn
2 squares of orange yarn

Step 1. Body

Back: Take 2 green squares and lay them on top of each other, matching the edges and corners. On one edge stitch a ¼-inch seam. Open. You have a rectangle 2 squares long and 1 square high.

Take two more green squares, lay them on top of each other, and stitch together on one edge with a ¼-inch seam. Open. You now have 2 rectangles of 2 squares each.

Lay the two green rectangles on top of each other, with right sides together, matching the seam lines, corners, and edges. Pin together along one long edge. Stitch a ¼-inch seam along the pinned long edge. Open. You now have a large green square consisting of 4 woven squares that is Twodot's back. Set aside.

Tummy: Take one orange square and one green square. Place the squares on top of each other, matching the corners and edges. Stitch together along 1 edge. Open into a rectangle. Repeat with the remaining orange square and another green square. You have 2 rectangles, each composed of 1 green and 1 orange square.

Lay the orange/green rectangles on top of each other, right sides together, so the orange squares are on top of the green squares, matching the edges, corners, and seam lines. Pin 1 long edge. Stitch a ¼-inch seam along pinned edge. Open. You now have a large square that alternates between green and orange squares. This is Twodot's tummy.

25

Fig. 1a

Fig. 1b

Fig. 1c

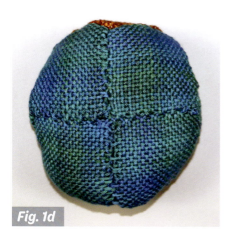
Fig. 1d

Fig. 1e

Lay the green large square on a flat surface, with right side up. Rotate the orange/green square into a diamond shape. Lay the orange/green square on top of the solid green square, with right sides together, so that the corners of the orange/green square are lined up with the seam lines on the solid green square. (See Fig. 1a.) Pin the corners of the orange/green square to the seam lines on the large green square, so the corner points match the edge of the green square at the seams. Now match the corner points of the solid green square to the seam lines and edges on the orange/green square. (See Fig. 1b.) Pin the corners.

Pin the straight edges of the squares together between the pinned points, matching the edges of the bottom squares to the edges of the top squares. (See Fig. 1c.) Once all the edges of the large green square and the large green/orange square are pinned together, stitch a ¼-inch seam around all edges, starting about ¾ inch from a point of one of the orange squares and ending seam about ¾ inch away from the point where you started stitching. This leaves a small 1½-inch opening on one edge for inserting stuffing and placing the head. Turn the squares right side out through the seam opening. This is Twodot's body.

Stuff the body through the seam opening to your desired firmness, shaping the body so the solid green back is rounded and the green/orange tummy is flatter.(See Figs. 1d and 1e.) The green tummy squares will now be the sides of the body. The 2 orange squares on the belly will be opposite each other— the inspiration for Twodot's name. The opening used for stuffing will be where the head is placed. The final body shape, after stuffing, should be an oval-shaped dome, with the green tummy squares wrapping over the long side of the oval and orange tummy squares at the narrow ends of the oval. Set the body aside.

Step 2. Head

Take 1 green square and, leaving a short beginning tail, stitch a running stitch around the entire outside edge about ¼ inch from the edge, rounding past the corners of the square. Pull on the ends of the running stitch to gather the edges to start forming a little bag. Put some stuffing into the bag and pull on the gathering yarn ends until you have an opening about 1 inch across. Knot the gathering thread ends together. Trim the gathering thread ends close to knot. Add or subtract stuffing to the head until you get your desired shape / size / firmness.

Place the head opening over the opening on the body where you inserted the stuffing, tucking the opening on the head into the opening on the body. Slip stitch the edges of the head opening to the edges of the body opening, turning under raw / looped edges of the body opening as you go. Set the body aside.

Step 3. Legs

Fold 1 green square in half and stitch a ¼-inch seam across 1 short end and along the long edge. Turn right side out. On the open end, turn the top of the leg to the inside of the leg so the leg measures about 2 inches long from seamed end to the folded edge. Stuff the leg. Repeat with the remaining green squares for a total of 4 legs. (See Fig. 3a.)

Fig. 3a

Fig. 3b

Place Twodot so the belly (orange/green squares) side is up. Place the ends of the legs so they are centered on the seam line between the orange and green squares. Slip stitch the tops of the legs to body. (See Fig. 3b.)

Step 4. Face

Using the black yarn or embroidery floss, make 1 French knot on each side of the head for the eyes. To do this, thread your yarn needle and tie a knot on one end of the yarn. Poke your yarn needle into a space between the yarn interlacements on one side of the head and out the opposite side. Pull the yarn through the head so the knot on the end goes into the head. Now make a French knot by wrapping your yarn 4 times around the needle. Then, keeping a little tension of the wrapped yarn, insert your needle back into the head right next to where the yarn comes out of the head. Pull yarn through until you have a nice, tidy knot for one of the eyes. Now wrap the black yarn 4 times around the needle and poke the needle back through the head. Pull the yarn fairly taut, tie a knot close to the head, and cut the yarn right next to the knot. Poke the last knot back into the head. Using the same black yarn, use a split stitch to make Twodot's mouth.

You are done! Give Twodot a hug.

PROJECT 2
Pryor the Panda

THE PROJECTS

PRYOR THE PANDA is very similar in construction to Twodot the Turtle and is another good beginning pattern to make. Since pandas are mountain dwellers, and all Critters are named for locations in Montana that start with the same letter as the Critter, I decided to name my panda for the Pryor Mountains in southeastern Montana. This mountain range covers areas south of Billings, including part of the Crow Nation Indian Reservation, Custer National Forest, and private lands. A herd of wild horses live in these mountains, and it's believed they descend from horses that were taken from the Lewis and Clark expedition. Expedition member Nathanial Pryor was tasked with finding the horses (without success). The expedition referred to the area as Pryor's Mountains, and the name stuck.

Supplies Needed
64 yards of black DK or light worsted knitting yarn
72 yards of white DK or light worsted knitting yarn
Stuffing
Black felt for eyes and nose (face pattern pieces are in the appendix)
Black sewing thread and needle

Weave the squares as follows:
8 squares of black yarn
9 squares of white yarn

Step 1. Body

Refer to "Rounded Body" on page 18 for step-by-step photos for constructing the body.

Take two white squares and lay them on top of each other, matching the edges and corners. On one edge, stitch a ¼-inch seam. Open into a rectangle.

Take two more white squares, lay them atop each other, and stitch together on one edge. Open. You now have 2 white rectangles composed of 2 squares each. Lay the 2 rectangles on top of each other, with right sides together, matching the seamlines, corners, and edges. Stitch ¼-inch seam along one long edge. Open. You now have a large square composed of 4 white squares. This is the Panda's tummy. Set aside.

Now stitch together 2 black squares to make a solid black rectangle. Stitch together 2 white squares into a solid white rectangle. Open both rectangles and lay on top of each other, with right sides together. Stitch a ¼-inch seam along one long edge. Open. You now have a large square with 2 black squares on one side and 2 white squares on the opposite side. The black squares will be the shoulders of the panda, and the white squares the lower back / bum.

Pryor's body is assembled in the same way as Twodot's body in Project 1. Lay the black/white square (Pryor's back) on a flat surface, with the right side up and the black shoulder squares at the upper edge of the square. Turn the all-white belly square so that it is a diamond shape, and lay it on top of the black/white square, with right sides together.

Pin the four corner points of the large white square to the

29

four seam lines of the black/white square, matching the tip of the points to the edges. Now pin the corner points of the black/white square to the seam lines on the white square, matching the corner tips to the edges. Match and pin the straight edges of the squares together between the pinned points, all the way around the body. Stitch a ¼-inch seam all around the body, leaving a small 1½-inch opening between the start and finish of the seam to insert stuffing.

Turn the body through the seam opening so the right sides are out. Stuff the body firmly and shape into a nice oval shape. Turn under the edges of the seam opening and slip stitch the seam opening closed. Set the body aside.

Step 2. Head

For the head, you will be doing a smaller 2-square version of the large squares used for the body. Lay 1 white square on your work surface. Turn a second white square into a diamond shape and place it on the first square so the points on the top square are centered between the corner points of the bottom square. (See Fig. 2a.)

Pin the points of the top square to the edges of the bottom square, centering the top square points between the points on the bottom square. Now pin the points of the bottom square to the top square so the bottom points are centered between the points of the top square. Match and pin edges of squares between the pinned points. Stitch a ¼-inch seam around all the edges, leaving a small

Fig. 2a

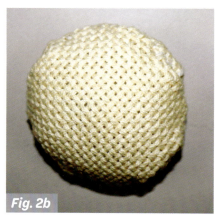

Fig. 2b

opening between the start and finish of the seam. Turn the head right side out through the seam opening and stuff firmly, forming into a squarish pillow. (See Fig. 2b.) Set the head aside.

Step 3. Ears

You will use 1 black square for each ear. Take a black square and fold 1 edge down 1 inch. Fold the opposite edge over so that the looped edge matches the fold and you have a small rectangle. Whip stitch through the loops on both short ends, and slip stitch through the loops on the long looped edge to the folded edge. Repeat with a second black square.

Fold one ear into a "U" shape, with the long stitched edge toward the back. Slip stitch the back edges together on the inside of the "U," leaving the front edges (folded side) open to shape the inside of the ear. The stitched back of the ear will be flat, and the front will have a little "divot" in the center like a panda's ear! Repeat with second ear.

Place the bottom of the ears on the top of the head, with about 1 inch between the inside edges of the ears. Using black yarn, slip stitch the bottom of the ears to the head around all ear bottom edges. Refer to the main project photo for the ears' placement.

Step 4. Nose and Face

Take the remaining white square and fold it into a triangle. Starting the seam 1 inch from the fold, stitch a ¼-inch seam along one edge, ending the seam 1 inch from the top point of the triangle. Now stitch straight across that top point, then continue stitching a ¼-inch seam down the remaining edge, ending 1 inch from the fold. (See Fig. 4a.)

Turn the triangle right side out through one of the side openings. The flattened point is the tip of the nose, and the two flaps will become the side of the nose. (See Fig. 4b.) Place a little stuffing into the point of the nose. Now push those side flaps into the inside of the nose so you have a folded edge on each side and each side of the nose measures about 1 inch along the folded-in sides. Add more stuffing if necessary to shape nose. Slip

THE PROJECTS

Fig. 4a

Fig. 4b

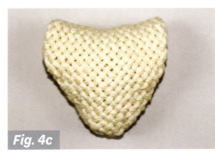
Fig. 4c

stitch the folded edges together on each side so the point of the nose is centered. The back of the nose should be about 1¼ inches wide side to side and about ¾ inch deep after stuffing. (See Fig. 4c.)

Place the nose on the head, with the bottom of the nose at the bottom of the head and the nose centered between the ears. Slip stitch back edges of the nose to the head all the way around the edges. (Refer to the main project photo for placement.)

Place the head on top of the body, with the nose on the same side as the white belly. The black/white side of the body is the panda's back, with the black squares as the upper body / shoulders, and the white squares are the lower body / bum. Slip stitch the bottom edges of the head to the top of the body. Set the body aside.

Step 5. Legs

You have 4 black squares remaining. Fold 1 of the squares in half and whip stitch through the loops across one short edge and then the long edge. Turn right side out through the open end and stuff firmly. Pinch the edges of the opening together so the long seam is centered in the opening. Whip stitch through the loops to close the end opening. Repeat with the remaining 3 black squares.

(Refer to the "Basic Legs" on page 19 for step-by-step photos.)

Place the upper legs on the body so the flat end of the leg matches the edge of the black squares on the shoulders and the seam on the leg is facing down. Slip stitch the top of the leg to the body where the leg edges touch the body. To make the feet, pinch the leg about 1 inch from the end. Stitch through the pinch fold to the bottom of the foot for a couple of stitches to secure the foot. (Refer to the main project photo for placement on the body.)

Place the lower legs on each side at the bottom of the body, so the legs keep the panda upright. Slip stitch around all leg edges that are touching the body. Make feet so the "toes" point upward.

Step 6. Face Details

Cut the eyes and nose out of black felt, using the Pryor the Panda face patterns in the appendix. Place the eyes on the face and, using a sewing needle / thread, slip stitch the edges of the eyes to the face. Do the same for the nose. Use a bit of your leftover black yarn or embroidery floss to embroider the mouth, using an outline stitch or split stitch. Set aside.

Pryor is ready to visit the mountains!

PROJECT 3
Shelby and Sidney the Sheep

THE PROJECTS

BOTH SHELBY AND SIDNEY are made from the same pattern, just changing the yarn colors. I like to say that the sheep are "low pressure" Critters. If your squares aren't perfectly woven or your seams are a bit wonky, that's okay because the fleece is going to cover everything up!

Shelby the Sheep is named for the town of Shelby, which is located on the north central plains of Montana, on the western end of what Montanans call "The High Line," where Highway 2 crosses the state for 670 miles from North Dakota to the Idaho border. This is an area to appreciate the Big Sky of Montana. The land is very flat and dominated by huge farms and ranch grazing lands. If you take the Amtrak Empire Builder train route from the east to Seattle, there is a stop in Shelby, so you can check it out!

Sidney the Sheep is named for the town of Sidney. If you drive east from Shelby for 401 miles, you will arrive in Sidney. Montanans generally describe distance in drive time rather than in actual miles, so this trip would be about six and a half hours, give or take, as we like to say.

Supplies Needed

- 72 yards black *or* white DK or light worsted knitting yarn
- 22 yards lumpy / bumpy textured knitting yarn for the fleece
- 2 12-inch-long pipe cleaners to stiffen the legs
- 1-inch-wide by 4-inch-long piece of cardboard or 1-inch-wide ruler to make fleece pom-poms
- Stuffing

Weave the squares as follows:

9 squares of black or white yarn

Step 1. Body

Take 2 of your squares and lay them on top of each other, matching the corners and edges. Stitch a ¼-inch seam on one edge. On the opposite edge, stitch a ¼-inch seam. You now have a tube open on opposite ends. This is the back / belly / sides of the sheep's body. Leave the tube wrong side out.

(Refer to "Small Closed Body Tube" on page 20 for step-by-step photos for constructing the body.)

Now take a third square and place it in one of the open ends of the tube, with the right sides together, matching one point of the square to one of the tube seam lines so that the square's point is about ½ inch above the edge of the tube. Pin. On the opposite side of the square, match the point to the other seam line on the tube, again

placing the point about ½ inch above the edge of the tube. Match the remaining points, on opposite sides, to the halfway point on each side of the tube; again, ½ inch of the point is above the edge of the tube. Pin. Match / pin the edges of the square to edge of the tube between the pinned points. Stitch a ¼-inch seam around the square / end of tube, easing in any excess fabric on the square and rounding the seam past the points. If you have some gathers in this seam, it doesn't matter! You will be covering the body with fleece.

Repeat on the other end of the tube, but this time, leave a small opening between the start and end of the seam. The single squares on each end of the tube are the chest and bum of the body.

Turn the body through the seam opening so the right side is out. Stuff the body firmly so the chest and bum squares bulge out a bit. Turn under the edges of the seam opening and slip stitch the opening closed. Set the body aside.

Step 2. Legs

Lay 2 squares on top of each other, matching the corners / edges. Stitch a ¼-inch seam on one edge. Open. You have a rectangle composed of 2 squares. Lay the rectangle on a flat surface, with the wrong side up.

Fold one pipe cleaner in half. Lay the folded pipe cleaner on one long edge of the rectangle. Tightly roll the rectangle around the pipe cleaner until you reach the opposite side. Pin the edges of the rectangle to the rolled-up section. Slip

Fig. 3a

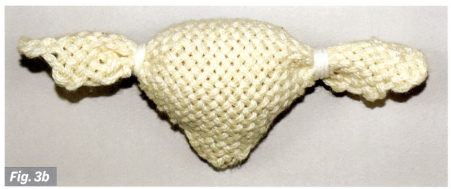

Fig. 3b

stitch through the loops across the end, then along the long edge and across the other end. Repeat these two steps for the second set of legs.

Position the front legs so the center seam on the leg matches one of the seams on the body and the front edge of the leg is next to the seam between the body and the chest. Slip stitch the front and back leg edges to the body for about 1 inch on each side of the leg seam (2 inches total). Repeat with the back legs, placing the back edge of the back legs at the bum / body seam.

Now bend the legs down at the spot where you started / ended stitching the legs to the body.

Adjust / rebend the legs until the sheep stands evenly. Slip stitch the tops of the bends in the legs to the body. Set the body aside.

Step 3. Head

Take your remaining square and fold into a triangle. From one of the points on the folded edge, measure 1 inch along a looped edge and pin. Stitch a ¼-inch seam, starting from the pin, down the edge, and around the middle point of the triangle; continue along remaining looped edge, stopping 1 inch from the fold. (See Fig. 3a.) Turn the head right side out through one of the openings. The closed point will be the nose, and the open points will be the ears.

THE PROJECTS

Stuff the head through the ear openings to shape the nose / top of the head. Don't leave stuffing in the ear flaps. Pinch the open ear flaps close to the stuffing and wrap the same color yarn as the body squares 2 or 3 times around the base of the ear. Knot the wrapped yarn and trim ends. Repeat with other ear, adjusting the head stuffing if needed. Knot the yarn on the ear wrap on the same side of the head as you did for the first ear. Those knots will be the backside of the head. (See Fig. 3b.) Position the head on the body so the head is centered on the chest, the top of the head is even or slightly higher than the back of the body, and the knots at the bases of the ears are toward the body. Slip stitch the back of the head to the chest where they touch. Set the body aside.

Step 4. Fleece

The fleece is made up of 27 pom-poms that are not cut on the end to make loops of yarn. To make the pom-poms, take the yarn you've chosen for the fleece, leave a starting ½-inch tail, and wrap the yarn 8 times around the 1-inch-wide piece of cardboard or ruler, so the starting end and ending end are on the same edge. Don't cut the fleece yarn yet. Thread a yarn needle with a piece of yarn left over from weaving the squares. Slip the yarn needle between the cardboard and wraps of yarn. Pull the yarn down to where the cut end is at the edge of the ruler. Tie yarn tightly around the fleece wraps and secure with a knot. Trim the yarn by the knot and cut the fleece yarn on the other side of the tie you just made, leaving about a ½-inch tail. Do not cut the pom-pom loops! Slip the pom-pom off the cardboard.

Continue until you have 27 pom-poms. You can make more if you like, but be aware that if you have too many, the weight of the fleece could make it difficult for the sheep to stand!

All pom-poms are attached to the body at the tied end so the pom-poms fan out. Thread the yarn needle with the body yarn. Center the first pom-pom on the chest below the head and stitch the tie end of the pom-pom to the chest. Place and stitch 4 more pom-poms on the chest, with approximately 1 inch between the ties on the pom-poms. Stitch 4 more pom-poms, spaced evenly across the shoulders in a row lined up with the legs. Then attach a row of 6 pom-poms around the belly and back. The next row of 4 pom-poms lines up with the back legs. Then attach a row of 5 pom-poms around the bum at the body / bum seam line. The last pom-poms are for the bum end. Fluff up the pom-poms so the fleece loops cover the body.

Make a whole herd of sheep!

35

PROJECT 4
Harrison the Hedgehog

HARRISON THE HEDGEHOG is another "low pressure" project because, if your weaving or sewing isn't perfect, the "spikes" will cover any imperfections! Harrison is named for Fort Harrison (now a VA hospital complex and museum) located in Montana's capital city, Helena.

Supplies Needed

48 yards white DK weight knitting yarn

60 yards (40 yards for weaving squares plus 20 yards for making the spikes) DK or light worsted variegated knitting yarn, referred to as "colored" in instructions

2 yards black fingering-weight or black embroidery floss for face

1-inch-wide x 4-inch-long cardboard to make "spike" pom-poms

Stuffing

Weave the squares as follows:

5 squares of colored yarn

6 squares of white yarn

Step 1. Body

Take one white and one colored square and lay them on top of each other, matching the edges and corners. Stitch a ¼-inch seam on one edge. Open so the right side is up. Take another colored square and lay it on top of the white square. Match outside end edges and corners. Stitch a ¼-inch seam on outside end edge. Open. You now have a rectangle of 3 squares stitched together in this order: 1 colored, 1 white, 1 colored. Repeat to make a second rectangle of 3 squares in same square / colors configuration.

(Refer to "Large Tube" on page 22 for step-by-step photos for constructing the body.)

Lay the two rectangles on top of each other, with the right sides together, matching seam lines, corners, and edges. Stitch a ¼-inch seam on one long edge. Open and lay flat, with the right side up.

You now have a large rectangle consisting of 6 squares. There should be 2 colored squares stacked up on the left, 2 white squares stacked in the middle, and 2 colored squares stacked on the right.

Now fold the left-hand 2 colored squares end over end to match the edge to the right-hand edge with the other 2 colored squares, so that the right sides are together and the colored squares are on top of each other. Match the outside edges, seam lines, and corners of the colored squares and stitch a ¼-inch seam, joining the colored squares together. You now have a tube that is 3 squares across by 2 squares wide, consisting of 2 rows of colored squares next to each other and a single row of white squares. The white squares are Harrison's tummy, and the colored squares will be his back / sides. The right side of the fabric is inside the tube.

Take another colored square and place it inside the opening on one end of the tube so the right sides are together. Match one corner of the square to the seam line between the 2 rows of colored squares. Pin the point so the point sticks up about ½ inch above the edge of the tube. Line up the opposite corner of the square with the middle of the white square. Pin so the point extends ½ inch above the tube opening edge. Pin the remaining corners to opposite sides of the tube, so all points extend about ½ inch above the edge of the tube. Match / pin the edges of the square to the edges of the tube between the pinned points.

Stitch a ¼-inch seam around the edges of the square / tube opening, rounding the seam past the square's corners. This is Harrison's bum.

Turn the body right side out through the open end of the tube.

Stuff the body to your desired firmness. Using the colored yarn, stitch a running stitch around the opening about ¼ inch from the open edge of the tube, leaving a short yarn tail at the beginning and end. Pull the ends of the yarn like a drawstring to gather the edges. Completely close the opening and tie the gathering yarn ends into a knot. Trim gathering yarn ends close to the knot. The body end with the gathering stitch is the neck / chest. Shape the body into a cylinder shape. (See Fig. 1.) Set aside.

Fig. 2a

Fig. 2b

Fig. 2c

Fig. 1

Step 2. Head

Take two white squares and lay them on top of each other, matching the edges and corners. Pin 2 adjacent edges and stitch a ¼-inch seam starting at one corner, along the edge to the next corner, then turn and stitch along the next edge to the next corner. Turn right side out and firmly stuff the stitched point only. The stuffed part will be the hedgehog's nose. The open side is the head.

Place the head opening over the gathered end of the body, so the top point matches the seam line running the length of the body between the colored squares. Pin the point. Center the opposite point of the opening on the white belly squares. Pin the point to the belly. The side seams of the nose should be about ½ inch above the body seams between the white tummy and colored back squares. Pin the lower edges of the head to the body. (See Fig. 2a.)

Now unpin and fold back the top head point until you see the gathered edge of the body. Use the white yarn to slip stitch the edge of the fold to the front of the body. (See Fig. 2b.)

After stitching the fold line on the inside of the head, flip the flap back up to the top of the body, smooth out the edges, pin, and slip stitch the edges of the head through the loops to the body, starting on one side seam and then up over the top of the head to the opposite side. Before you continue slip stitching around the bottom of the head, adjust the nose / head stuffing if necessary. Continue slip stitching through the loops at the bottom edge of the head to the body. (See Fig. 2c.) Set the body aside.

Step 3. Legs

Take one white square (see Fig. 3a) and, starting at one corner, roll it tightly across to the opposite corner. (See Fig. 3b.) Secure the ending corner to the roll with a pin. Slip stitch all the looped edges through the loops to the rolled part of the leg. Whip stitch the loops on the points together to make a pointy "foot" on each side. Repeat with the last white square.

Place the front legs on the hedgehog's belly, centering the legs over the point on the underside of the head, with the stitched loops edge on the feet facing you. Slip stitch the edges of the front legs to

THE PROJECTS

Fig. 3a

Fig. 3b

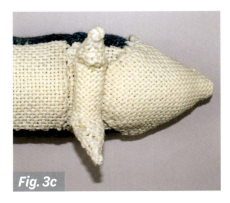

Fig. 3c

the belly where they touch, leaving the pointy feet free. (See Fig. 3c.) Place the back legs on the rear of the belly, with the back edge of the legs about ½ inch away from the bum / body seam. Slip stitch the edges of the back legs to the belly.

Step 4. Spikes

Harrison's "spikes" are made of 1-inch pom-poms from your colored yarn. To make the pom-poms, wrap your colored yarn 6 times around the piece of cardboard, starting and ending wraps on the same edge. Do not cut the yarn yet. Thread a length of colored yarn on the yarn needle. Slip the yarn needle under the loops of yarn and pull the yarn through until you have about a 2-inch tail by the wraps on the cardboard. Pull on each side of the yarn to move the yarn down to the edge, with the cut end of the yarn wraps. Tie the yarn tightly around the wraps, making sure to catch that cut end. Trim the yarn close to the knot. Cut the loops on the edge opposite the knot. You have pom-pom #1.

Make a total of 73 pom-poms. (Optional: make 2 more pom-poms for "bangs.") The pom-poms are whip stitched at the tied end of the pom-poms to the hedgehog's body. Place the pom-pom tie ends about ¾ inch from its neighbor's tie end and in rows across the body. The row placement / number of pom-poms per row is as follows:

Row 1: Place a row of 10 pom-poms across the top of the head between the side seam lines for the white belly and colored back / sides (Optional: Take the 2 extra pom-poms to create "bangs" and place front of the row of 10 pom-poms.)

Rows 2–8: Place 7 rows of 7 pom-poms each (49 total pom-poms) that run the length of the body from the back edge of the head to the seam line for the bum. The first row of pom-poms starts on the seam line between the white belly and the colored body squares. The last row is on the opposite side of the body at the belly / body seam line. Space the remaining rows evenly across the width of the body between the first 2 rows of pom-poms.

Rows 9–12: Place 4 rows of pom-poms on the bum, starting ½ inch above the bottom seam between white and colored squares in the following configuration:

- Bottom bum Row: 3 pom-poms
- Next bum row up: 5 pom-poms
- Next bum row up: 4 pom-poms
- Last bum row next to top seam: 2 pom-poms

Fluff the pom-poms so they stick out all over the place.

Step 5: Face

Thread some black yarn or embroidery floss onto your yarn needle. Stitch a nose, using embroidery satin stitch. Make 2 French knots for the eyes, wrapping the yarn 6 times around the needle.

Introduce your hedgehog to the world!

PROJECT 5
Alzada the Angora Goat

THE PROJECTS

ALZADA THE ANGORA GOAT is named for a tiny unincorporated town (population 25) in far southeastern Montana near the Wyoming and South Dakota borders. Alzada, the town, was originally established as a stagecoach stop in 1878.

Alzada's body is made exactly like the bodies of Shelby and Sidney the Sheep, so if the directions sound familiar, they are!

Supplies Needed

85 yards white DK weight knitting yarn
20 yards lumpy / bumpy textured yarn for the fleece
Stuffing
2 12-inch-long pipe cleaners
Piece of cardboard 3½ inches square for fleece pom-poms

Weave the squares as follows:

10 squares of white yarn

Refer to "Small Closed Body Tube" on page 20 for step-by-step photos.

Step 1. Body

Take 2 of your squares and lay them on top of each other, matching the corners and edges. Stitch a ¼-inch seam on one edge. On the opposite edge, stitch a ¼-inch seam. You now have a tube open on opposite ends. Leave the tube wrong side out.

Now take a third square and place it in one of the open ends, with the right sides together, matching one point to one of the tube seams so that the square's point is about ½ inch above the edge of the tube. Pin. On the opposite side of the square, match the point to the other seam on the tube, again placing the point about ½ inch above the edge of the tube. Match the remaining points, on opposite sides, to the halfway point on each side of the tube, and again ½ inch of the point is above the edge of the tube. Pin. Match / pin the edges of the square to the edge of the tube between the pinned points. Stitch a ¼-inch seam around the square / end of tube, easing in any excess fabric on the square and rounding the seam past the points. If you have some gathers in this seam, it doesn't matter! You will be covering the body with fleece.

Repeat on the other end of the tube, but this time leave a small opening between starting and ending the seam. The squares on each end of the tube are the chest and bum. Turn the body through the seam opening so the right side is out. Stuff the body firmly through the seam opening, so the chest and bum round out a bit. Turn under the edges of the seam opening and slip stitch the seam opening closed. This is the goat's body. Set aside.

Step 2. Legs

Lay 2 squares on top of each other, matching the corners / edges. Stitch a ¼-inch seam on one edge. Open. You have a rectangle composed of 2 squares. Lay the rectangle on your work surface, with the wrong side up.

Fold one pipe cleaner in half. Lay the folded pipe cleaner on one long edge of the rectangle. Tightly roll the rectangle around the pipe cleaner until you reach the opposite side. Pin the leg edge to the rolled-up section. Slip stitch through the loops across one narrow end, along the long edge, and across the other narrow end. Repeat these steps for the second set of legs.

Position the front legs so the center seam on the leg matches one of the seams on the body and the front edge of the leg is next to the seam for the chest. Slip stitch the edges of the leg to the body for about 1 inch on each side of the leg seam (2 inches total) on both the front and back edges of the leg. Repeat with the back leg, placing the back edge of the back legs at the bum / body seam.

Now bend the legs down at the spot where you started / ended, stitching the legs to the body. Adjust / rebend the legs until the goat stands evenly. Slip stitch the tops of the bends in the legs to the body. Set the body aside.

Step 3. Head and Neck

Head: Take 1 square and fold it into a triangle. From a point on the folded edge, measure out 1 inch along the looped edge of triangle. Pin. Stitch a ¼-inch seam, starting from that pin and around the middle point, and continue along the remaining edge to 1 inch away from the remaining point on the fold. (See Fig. 3a.) Turn the head right side out through one of the openings. The closed point will be the nose, and the open points will be the ears. (See Fig. 3b.)

Fig. 3a

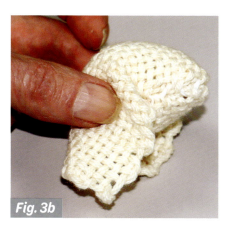
Fig. 3b

Stuff the closed point of the head, but don't put stuffing in the ear areas. Fold the ear flaps down from the back of the head so that the tips of the ears tips point down on each side of the head. Slip stitch the upper side edges of the ears to the head, so the ears stay in place with the tips pointing downward. Set aside.

Neck: Unlike the sheep, Alzada has a neck.

(Refer to "Neck Shape" on page 21 for step-by-step photos.)

Take the remaining white square and fold one corner down 1 inch and pin. With the folded corner on the outside, fold the square into a triangle. Stitch a ¼-inch seam along the edge from the fold out to the nearest corner. Turn the neck right side out and stuff it into a cone shape.

Center the neck on the front of the goat so the point on the large open end is centered on the back seam of the body. Center the neck seam line on the front of the chest. Slip stitch the bottom edge of the neck to the body through the loops, all the way around the neck edges. Adjust the neck stuffing as needed through the top opening of the neck.

Place the bottom of the head on the opening at the top of the neck. Slip stitch the bottom edge of the head to the folded edges of the small opening of the neck.

Step 4. Fleece

The fleece is made up of long pieces of textured yarn because Angora goats have wavy fleece. You can use a bulky weight smooth yarn if you prefer. Cut 29 pieces of fleece yarn, with each piece measuring 8 inches long. This is the first layer of fleece. Place the first piece of fleece centered on the body back seam and next to the seam line, where the back and bum meet. Pin at the center. Continue to lay and pin 19 more lengths (20 total) next to each other down the back of the goat, centering the lengths on the back of the goat and ending where the head and neck meet. Stitch the fleece to the body along the center back, using a backstitch that goes into the body, under the center of the length of fleece, then up. Then reinsert the tip of the needle into the same spot in which you started, so a loop of stitching yarn is around the fleece yarn. Have the needle exit on the other side of the next piece of fleece yarn. Repeat the backstitch for each piece of fleece until all are secured along the center back.

Fold the remaining 9 pieces of fleece in half and line them up across the top edge of the goat's bum, matching the fold to the body / bum seam line. Individually stitch each piece of fleece to the body at the fold.

Smooth all the lengths of fleece on both sides of the body and backstitch them to the sides of the goat about 1 inch down from the first line of stitching on the center of the back. This will help the first layer of fleece lie flat against the body.

For the second layer of fleece, cut a piece of cardboard 3½ inches square. Make 7 pom-poms of 3 wraps around the cardboard out of the fleece yarn, starting and ending at the bottom edge on the cardboard. Tie the pom-poms at the uncut end of the wraps, with extra white yarn threaded on the yarn needle. Slip the tip of the yarn needle between the wraps and cardboard, pull the yarn under the wraps, then pull the yarn up to the edge of the cardboard opposite the cut ends. Tie the yarn around the fleece with a knot. Trim the yarn tie ends by the knot and cut the textured fleece yarn opposite the tied end.

Center the tie on the pom-poms on the back of the body and space / pin them evenly down the back of the goat, starting at the seam between the bum / back. Your last pom-pom should be at the backside of the head. Stitch each pom-pom at the ties to the back of the goat, on top of the ties for the first layer of fleece. Drape the cut ends so that 3 pieces of yarn are on each side of the body and the pom-pom over the bum drapes over the bum.

Cut 4 lengths of textured yarn, each 4 inches long. Fold a piece in half and place the fold at the top of the neck, along the bottom edge of the head. Stitch the fold to the neck. Repeat with 3 remaining yarn lengths, spacing them around the top of the neck so the chest area is covered with fleece.

Cut 4 lengths of textured yarn, each 5 inches long. Fold each in half and place fold at the back of the head so the cut ends go forward over the head for bangs. Trim the bangs to the length you like. You can stitch the bangs to the head or let them hang free. Fluff up the fleece so it lies evenly.

Welcome Alzada to your herd!

PROJECT 6
Libby the Llama

THE PROJECTS

LIBBY THE LLAMA is named for the town of Libby, located in far northwestern Montana. For decades, the Libby area was host to vermiculite mines, and many residents worked at the mines. However, the vermiculite in the Libby area had a very high content of asbestos, which led to deadly consequences. After years of struggles and determined advocacy, the area was declared a Federal Superfund site, and cleanup of the environmental damage was completed in 2015. The people of Libby are tough, resilient, and defenders of their community—a lot like llamas!

Libby's body and neck are made like Alzada the goat and the sheep.

Supplies Needed

- 80 yards white DK weight yarn
- 55 yards light worsted colored yarn for fleece (I used a wool / mohair blend yarn that gives the fleece nice drape and a little shine.)
- Stuffing
- Black fingering weight yarn or embroidery floss for the face
- 2 pieces of cardboard to make pom-poms for fleece—one piece 4 inches square and another piece 3 inches square

Weave the squares as follows:

10 squares in white DK weight yarn

Step 1. Body

(Refer to "Closed Body Tube" on page 20 for step-by-step photos for constructing the body.)

Take 2 of your squares and lay them on top of each other, matching the corners and edges. Stitch a ¼-inch seam on one edge. On the opposite edge, stitch a ¼-inch seam. You will now have a tube open on opposite sides. Leave the tube wrong side out.

Now take a third square and place it into one of the open tube ends, with the right sides together, matching one square point to one of the tube seams so that the point is about ½ inch above the edge of the tube. Pin. On the opposite side of the square, match the point to the other seam on the tube, again so the point is about ½ inch above the edge of the tube. Pin. Match the remaining points to the center on each side of the tube between the pinned points; again, ½ inch of the points are above the edge of the tube. Pin the points. Match and pin the edges of the square to the tube edges between pinned points. Stitch a ¼-inch seam around the square / end of the tube, rounding the seam past the points and easing in any excess fabric on the square. This will be the llama's bum. If you have some gathers in this seam, it doesn't matter! You will be covering the body with fleece. Repeat these instructions with another square in the other end of the tube, but this time, leave a small opening between starting and ending the seam. This end is the llama's chest.

Turn the body through the seam opening so the right side is out. Stuff the body firmly, so the bum and chest squares bulge out a bit. Turn under the edges of the opening and slip stitch the opening closed. Set the body aside.

Step 2. Head

Take one square and fold it into a triangle. Stitch a ¼-inch seam around the open point of the triangle, starting and ending 1 inch from the fold on each side. (See Fig. 2a.) The openings will be Libby's ears. Turn the head right side out through one of the ear openings. Stuff the stitched point of the head firmly.

Fig. 2a

45

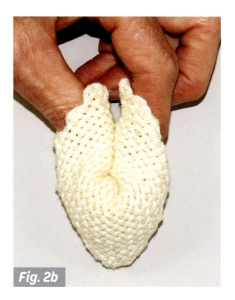

Fig. 2b

Fig. 2c

Fig. 2d

With the head facing you, insert your thumb / pointer finger in the ear openings on each side and pinch the ears together so the inside edges meet over the top of the head. (See Fig. 2b.) Hold the ears firmly and turn the head so you are looking at the seam line. Poke a finger against the bottom of the head to push the stuffing and fabric up into the head. (See Fig. 2c.) Stitch the bases of the ears together with a Tacking stitch. Slip stitch the edges of the fold created on the bottom of the head together.

Fold the ears upright and toward the center back of the head. Slip stitch the edges of the fold created at the base of the ears to the top of the head. Do not cut the yarn yet. Adjust the ears so the insides of the ears face forward. Push your needle from the fold you just stitched, through the backside of the top of the head, to the other side of the ear. Make sure the ear is facing forward and add a small stitch through the base of the ear to the back of the head to keep the ear upright. Repeat for the second ear. Knot the yarn and hide the knot between the ears on the back of the head. Trim the stitching yarn close to the knot. (See Fig. 2d.)

Step 3. Neck

Take another square and fold one corner down 1 inch. Now fold it into a triangle shape, with the folded point on the outside. Stitch a ¼-inch seam from the folded edge to the point. Turn it right side out. Stuff the neck firmly into a cone shape.

(Refer to "Neck Shape" on page 21 for step-by-step photos.)

The seam lines on the body are the center of the back and center of the belly. Place the large open end of the neck on the body, so the neck seam matches the body back seam and the point opposite the neck seam is centered on the chest. Pin the edges of the neck to the body and slip stitch through the loops at the edge of the neck to the body. Adjust the stuffing, if needed, through the opening on the top of the neck, so the neck stands erect. Place the head on the small opening at the top of the neck and slip stitch the bottom of the head to the folded edge at the neck top all the way around the neck opening. Set the body aside.

Step 4. Legs

(Refer to "Cone" on page 21 for step-by-step photos for constructing the legs.)

Fold a square into a triangle and stitch a ¼-inch seam along one edge, from the fold to the top point. Turn it right side out and stuff it firmly into a cone shape. This is one leg. Repeat with 3 more squares for 4 legs total.

Position the front legs on the body so that the open end point is centered on the seam where the chest and body meet and the leg seam is in line with the body seam on the belly. Pin the leg edges to the body and slip stitch through the loops around the top of the leg to attach the leg to the body, adjusting the stuffing as necessary. Repeat on the other side of the body for the other front leg, making sure the legs are the same length on each side. (Refer to the main photo of Libby for placement.)

Position the back leg so the open point on the leg is centered on the seam between the body squares and the bum square and the leg seam is even with the seam on the belly. Pin and slip stitch through the loops on the top of the back leg to the body, adjusting the stuffing as necessary. Make sure the leg is the same length as the front legs. Repeat on the other side for the other back leg.

Step 5. Fleece

The fleece is made from your colored yarn and consists of layers of long pom-poms. You will need 2 pieces of cardboard to wind the yarn around. One piece of cardboard needs to be 4 inches square, and the second piece of cardboard is 3 inches square. To secure the yarn pom-poms, thread some colored fleece yarn onto the yarn needle. After winding the number of wraps designated for the different pom-poms (see below), slip the needle between the wraps of yarn and the cardboard, then pull the yarn through, leaving a small tail. Pull the yarn to the end of the pom-pom without a cut end and tie the yarn on the needle tightly around the wraps at the edge of the cardboard. Cut tie yarn close to the knot. Cut the pom-pom wraps on the side opposite the tie. Trim the starting and ending wrap ends to match the length of the other yarn lengths in the pom-pom.

Back fleece pom-poms: Make 6 pom-poms by wrapping the colored fleece yarn 10 times around the 4-inch cardboard. Cut the wraps on the edge opposite the tie end, securing the yarns. Open and evenly place / pin the pom-poms at the ties on the back, with the ties centered on the seam line, with the first pom-pom at the seam line of the bum / body and the last pom-pom at the base of the neck. Once you are pleased with the spacing, slip stitch the pom-poms to the llama's back through the pom-pom ties. This is the first layer of fleece.

Second layer of back fleece: Make 6 pom-poms by wrapping the colored yarn 10 times around the 3-inch piece of cardboard. Open and lay the pom-pom ties between the pom-poms of the first layer of fleece. Pin and slip stitch the pom-poms to the body at the ties.

Bum fleece: Make 3 pom-poms by wrapping colored yarn 5 times around the 3-inch cardboard. The first pom-pom goes at the top of the bum, and the others line up across the bum below the first pom-pom. Stitch the pom-poms to the bum at the tie end.

Chest fleece: Make 6 pom-poms by wrapping colored yarn 10 times around the 3-inch cardboard. Evenly place these pom-poms on the chest, with the cut ends hanging down so the fleece covers the chest area.

If desired, trim the ends of the pom-poms so the fleece ends are fairly even around the body.

Step 6. Face

Using black fingering weight yarn or embroidery floss, make a French knot on each side of the head up near the base of the ears on each side of the head. Knot and cut the yarn right next to the head. To make eyelashes, make a knot about ½ inch from one end of the black yarn. Push your needle through the head, starting just above one of the eyes and exiting just above the opposite eye. Pull the yarn tight, so the first knot is snug against the head. Tie another knot above the other eye very close to the fabric. Trim the yarn end to ½ inch. Unply the cut ends and trim to about a ¼-inch eyelash length.

Libby is ready to guard your Swatch Critter herd.

PROJECT 7
Eureka the Unicorn

EUREKA is named for the town of Eureka, located in the far northwest corner of Montana, just south of the Canadian border. It's tough to find a town, river, or other natural feature that starts with the letter "U" in Montana. But in "Eureka," the "E" is silent. And it perfectly expressed my feeling of "Eureka! I made a unicorn!"

Eureka's body and neck are made exactly like Libby the Llama's.

Supplies Needed

80 yards white DK weight knitting yarn

17 yards colored DK weight yarn for mane / tail

3-inch piece of pipe cleaner

1 yard of gold metallic cording or yellow fingering weight yarn

Stuffing

3-inch square and 5-inch square pieces of cardboard to make pom-poms for mane / tail

Weave the squares as follows:

10 squares of white yarn

Refer to the special section for step-by-step photos for making the body ("Small Closed Body Tube," page 20), the neck ("Neck Shape," page 21), and the legs ("Cone," page 21).

Step 1. Body

Take 2 squares and lay them on top of each other, matching the corners and edges. Stitch a ¼-inch seam on one edge. On the opposite edge, stitch a ¼-inch seam. You will now have a tube open on opposite sides. Leave the tube wrong side out.

Now take a third square and place it into one of the open ends of the tube, with the right sides together, matching one point of the square to one of the tube seams, with the point about ½ inch above the edge of the tube. Pin. On the opposite side of the square, match the point to the other seam on the tube so the point is about ½ inch above the edge of the tube. Center the remaining points of the square between the pinned points, and again, with ½ inch of the point above the edge of the tube. Pin. Match / pin the edges of the square / tube opening between the pinned points. Stitch a ¼-inch seam

around the square / end of the tube, easing in any excess fabric on the square and rounding seam past the points.

Repeat on the other end of the tube, but leave a small opening between starting and ending the seam. The squares on the ends of the tube are the chest and bum.

Turn the body through the seam opening so the right side is out. Stuff the body firmly so the bum and chest squares bulge out a little. The tube seams are the center back and center belly of the body. Turn the edges of the seam opening under and slip stitch the seam opening closed. This is the unicorn's body. Set aside.

Step 2. Neck

Take another square and fold one point down ½ inch. Fold the square into a triangle shape, with the folded point on the outside. Stitch a ¼-inch seam from fold edge to point. Turn right side out. The folded back end is the top of the neck. Stuff the neck firmly all the way from small opening to the edge of the large opening.

Place the large opening of the neck on the body, so the neck seam matches the back body seam and the point is centered on the chest. Pin the edges of the large opening to the chest, then slip stitch through the loops at the large opening of the neck to the front of the chest, adjusting the stuffing as needed. Refer to the main project photo for neck placement on the chest and body.

Step 3. Head

The head starts with the same shape as the neck. Take one square and fold one corner down ¾ inch. Fold the square into a triangle, with the folded point on the outside and matching the looped edges. Stitch a ¼-inch seam from the folded edge out to the point of the triangle, so you have a cone shape with a small opening on one end and a large opening on the opposite end. Turn it right side out.

The narrow end of the cone is the nose end of the head. Center the seam in the middle of the cone shape. Slip stitch the folded edges of the narrow end of the cone together. Stuff the head firmly. The seam side of the cone shape is the underside of head. (See Fig. 3a.)

On the open end of the head, fold the point over the stuffing toward the seam side of the head, so the looped edges meet, and pin the point to the seam line. The two new points created by folding the square's point over the top of the stuffing are the ears. Pinch one ear point and wrap white yarn around the base of the ear, about ½ inch in from the outside edge of the ear point. Pull the wrapping yarn tight and secure it with a knot. (See Fig. 3b.) Repeat these steps for the other ear. Adjust the

Fig. 3b

Fig. 3a

head stuffing, if necessary, and check that the looped edges of the pinned flap / back of the head between the ears still meet. Starting from one ear, slip stitch the looped edges of the flap and back of the head together, ending at the opposite ear. Now, insert the tip of your needle at the base of one ear and push the needle through the head, exiting at the wraps at the base of the opposite ear. Pull the yarn tight to shape the head, and secure with a knot. Cut the yarn close to the knot. (See Fig. 3c.)

Place the head on the top opening of the neck, so the side of the head with seams is against the neck opening. Slip stitch the folded edges of the neck top to the bottom of the head.

Step 4. Legs

Back legs: Take a square and fold it into a triangle. Stitch a ¼-inch seam along one edge from fold to point. Turn it right side out into a cone shape. This is one *back* leg. Repeat with another square. Stuff the legs firmly.

Front legs: Fold a square into a triangle, but stitch the seam starting at a ¼-inch seam on the fold edge, and angle the seam to be a 1-inch seam at the point. Turn it right side out and stuff firmly. Repeat with another square.

Position the front legs on the body so the point on the opening is centered on the seam line where the chest and body meet and the leg seam is in line with the body seam on the belly. Pin the leg opening to the body and check to make

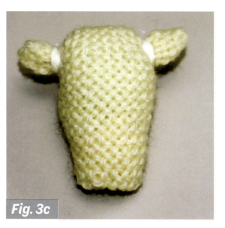
Fig. 3c

sure the legs are the same length. Slip stitch through the loops the top edges of the leg to the body.

Position the back legs so the point on the leg is centered on the seam between the body, the bum, and the leg seam, even with the seam on the belly. Pin the leg edges and slip stitch the top edges of the leg to the body through the loops, making sure all the legs are the same length.

Step 5. Horn

The horn is made with a 3-inch length of pipe cleaner wrapped with the metallic thread or yarn of your choice. Fold the pipe cleaner piece in half. Measure 1 inch down from the fold and fold the cut ends out. The pipe cleaner should look like a capital "T" turned upside down with the bottom of the "T" as the point on the horn and the folded-out crossbar is the bottom of the horn.

Thread the metallic cord on your yarn needle. Do not knot the end of the yarn. Place one end of the metallic cord in the fold in the pipe cleaner at the tip of the horn. Warp the cord a couple of times over the tip of the horn fold, so the folded tip is covered, then firmly squeeze together the fold of the pipe cleaner. Now tightly wrap the length of the pipe cleaner with the metallic cord, so the pipe cleaner is completely covered by the metallic yarn, and you reach the crossbar of the "T." Secure the end of the metallic thread, either with a bit of glue or by threading the end of the cord onto the yarn needle, and insert the needle tip into the wrapped horn and out between the wraps about halfway up. Cut the metallic cord close to the horn.

Bend the unwrapped pipe cleaner ends so they make a shallow "V," and insert the ends into the forehead.

Step 6. Mane and Tail

The mane and tail are both long pom-poms.

For the tail: Wrap your colored yarn 12 times around the 5-inch square piece of cardboard, starting and ending on the same edge of the cardboard. Thread the yarn needle with a piece of the tail yarn and slip the tip of the needle between the yarn wraps and cardboard. Pull the yarn on the needle up to the edge of the cardboard, opposite the edge where you started the wraps. Tie the yarn tightly around the pom-pom wraps and trim the tie yarn close to the knot. Cut the yarn warps on the opposite end of the pom-pom from the tie. You now have a tail consisting of 24 lengths of yarn, each 5 inches long. To make the tail curly, insert the tip of your yarn needle between the plies of yarn and unravel all the yarn lengths. Position the tie end of the tail at the top of the bum at the body back seam / bum seam. Stitch the top of the tail to the body.

For the mane: Make 5 pom-poms. Wrap your colored yarn 6 times around a 3-inch piece of cardboard. Tie one end of the pom-pom and cut the other end. This makes 1 pom-pom with 12 lengths of yarn. Make 4 more pom-poms. Place the first mane pom-pom on the back of the head, then place three more pom-poms spaced evenly down the neck. Stitch the pom-poms to the neck at the ties. Take the 5th pom-pom and place the tie between the ears so the cut ends go toward the nose. This is the forelock. Stitch the forelock to the head at the tie end. Unravel the lengths of yarn to make the mane and forelock curly. Smooth the mane, tail, and forelock into place, trimming any yarn that you feel is too long.

Share some unicorn magic!

PROJECT 8
Delphia the Fiber Fairy

THE PROJECTS

DELPHIA THE FIBER FAIRY is named for a "population concentration" north of the town of Round Up in south-central Montana. Delphia was a town with a post office until 1959. Now the former townsite is a small collection of deserted buildings in a rural ranching area. Some may consider Delphia a "ghost town," but I like to think that fairies inhabit the area instead of ghosts. Delphia is the only Critter that breaks my "name starts with the same letter as the Critter" rule, because Delphia struck me as a lovely fairy's name.

One note to remember for Delphia: when stitching the seams, match the color of the stitching yarn to the color of the squares being seamed.

Supplies Needed

25 yards magenta DK or light worsted knitting yarn

50 yards variegated DK or light worsted knitting yarn

16 yards black DK or light worsted knitting yarn

8 yards white DK or light worsted knitting yarn

4 12-inch pipe cleaners

2-inch square piece of cardboard

Stuffing

Weave the squares as follows:

3 squares of magenta yarn

2 squares of black yarn

1 square of white yarn

6 squares of variegated DK knitting yarn (extra yarn is used for Delphia's hair)

Step 1. Body

Take 1 magenta square and fold in half, matching the corners / edges. Stitch a ¼-inch seam along the long edge. Turn right side out. The seam will be at the back of the body. Leave both ends open and stuff. Do a running stitch around one open end, ¼ inch away from the edge, starting and ending at the seam. Leave a 2-inch tail. Set the body aside.

Step 2. Head

Take the white square and stitch a running stitch drawstring ¼ inch from the edges all the way around the square, rounding stitching past the corners. Leave short yarn tails at the beginning and end. Draw the stitching tight enough to make a little bag with an opening large enough to insert stuffing. Stuff the head firmly. Pull the drawstring tight, closing the head opening completely, and knot the drawstring yarn ends. Trim the ends close to the knot. The gathered end is the neck. You can leave the head round or shape the head into an oval by pinching the back of the head to make a tuck / dart and slip stitching the two edges of the tuck together. Don't worry about this tuck being smooth, because the hair will cover this part of the head.

Insert the gathered neck end of the head into the body end where you sewed the gathering stitch. Pull the gathering stitch yarn ends on the body until the body opening fits around the neck. Tie the body gathering stitch ends together in a knot and trim yarn close to knot. Slip stitch the bottom of the head to the inside of the neck opening of the body.

Step 3. Arms

The other two magenta squares are the arms. Fold one square into a triangle and stitch a ¼-inch seam on one side, from folded edge to point. Turn right side out. Repeat with the remaining magenta square. You have 2 cone shapes for the arms / sleeves.

(Refer to "Cone" on page 21 for step-by-step photos for constructing the arms.)

Take one arm and fold it so the seam is centered between the small end point and the center point on the wider open end. On the narrow end, fold the stitched

53

point down ½ inch, matching the seam line on the point to the seam line on the rest of the arm. Tack the point down with a single stitch, catching only the seamed layer of the sleeve / arm. This narrow end becomes the shoulder. Repeat with the last magenta square so you have 2 arms.

Take one of the pipe cleaners and insert one end into the open end of an arm, then poke that end of the pipe cleaner through the center of the fold at the narrow shoulder end of the arm. Now, holding the body with the head up and the back seam away from you, poke the same end of the pipe cleaner through the body, just below the gathers at neck / head. Take the second arm and poke the same end of the pipe cleaner through the narrow shoulder end of the second arm, then out into the open end of the second arm. Adjust the pipe cleaner so you have equal lengths in each arm.

Push the shoulders of the arms against the edges of the body on each side, so the folded edge is just below the gathering yarn line at the top end of the body. Make sure the seams on the arms are next to the sides. Slip stitch the top of the arms to the body around all edges where they touch, so it looks like the top of a sleeve.

Once you have the arms attached to the body, fold each end of the pipe cleaner back so the end of the fold barely shows out the end of the sleeve. Twist the pipe cleaner end to the rest of the pipe cleaner to form a little loop for a hand. Set the body aside.

Step 4. Legs

Lay the 2 black squares on top of each other, matching the edges and corners. Stitch a ¼-inch seam along one edge. Open it into a rectangle and lay it on a flat surface, with the wrong side up. Fold a pipe cleaner in half, place it on one long edge of the rectangle, and roll the squares tightly around the pipe cleaner until you get to the other side of the rectangle. Pin the looped edge of the rectangle to the rolled part of the leg, and slip stitch the looped edge to the rolled part of the leg. Slip stitch each end closed, so the leg ends are slightly pointed for feet.

Bend the legs into a "V" at the seam line between the squares and place the point of the "V" in the opening at the bottom of the body, making sure the slip stitched leg edge is facing toward the back. Slip stitch the edges of the bottom of the body to the top of the legs all the way around the body opening / top of legs.

Fig. 5

Step 5. Skirt

The skirt is made from 2 squares of the variegated colored yarn. Fold each square in half at an angle so the points are offset. Lay the folded edges of the squares on top of each other, and adjust the points so they line up from front skirt square to back skirt square. Pin and slip stitch the folded edges together, leaving a 2-inch opening in the center. The opening is the waistband of the skirt. (See Fig. 5.)

Insert the legs / bottom of the body into the waistline opening of the skirt, so the folded edges of the skirt are about 1 inch above where the legs / body are sewn together. Make sure the seams on each side of the skirt's waistband are at the sides of the body. Pin the skirt waistline to body and slip stitch the waistline folded edges of the skirt to the body, all the way around. Set the body aside.

Step 6. Wings

The wings are made like the arms. Take a variegated colored square and fold it into a triangle. Whip stitch through the loops on one edge from fold to point. Flatten it into a cone shape by centering the seam side over the point side, similar to the sleeves. Repeat 3 more times for a total of 4 wings.

Take a pipe cleaner and fold it in half to mark the center, then open. About 1½ inches from that bend, make another bend of about 45 degrees. Now bend the rest of that end of the pipe cleaner into a triangle, so that each side measures about 1 inch. To secure the triangle shape, wrap the end of the pipe cleaner around the long starting length of pipe cleaner just below the first bend for the triangle. (See Fig. 6a.)

Insert the straight end of the pipe cleaner into the wide end of one of the wing cones, and poke the pipe cleaner end through the small point at the end of the cone. (See Fig. 6b.) Take a second wing cone shape and poke the end of the pipe cleaner through the narrow end and out the wide opening end. Fold this end of the pipe cleaner into the triangle shape used on the first side of the wing. Adjust the wings so the narrow points meet on the pipe cleaner, the seams are on the same side, and the triangles on the ends of the pipe cleaner are enclosed in the seamed end of the wings, with the flat outer end of the triangle matching the flat edge of the open end of the wing cone. Slip stitch the open flat edge of the cone to the pointed layer of the wing, catching the pipe cleaner a few times on each wing. Stitch the wings together at the narrow ends, again catching the pipe cleaner at least once. (See Fig. 6c.) Repeat with the other 2 wing cones. You have 2 sets of wings.

Step 7. Attaching the Wing

Lay the 2 sets of wings next to each other on a flat surface, with the seam sides down on both sets of wings and the wing center points matching. Slip stitch the inner folded edges of the wing sets together for ½ inch at the center points. Place the wings on the back of the fairy, so the seam sides of the wings are toward the back. Stitch the wing edges to the body.

Step 8. Hair

The hair is a single pom-pom. Wrap the remaining variegated colored yarn around the 2-inch square piece of cardboard 30 times, starting and ending on the same edge of the cardboard. Thread a piece of scrap colored yarn on the yarn needle; slide the needle between the cardboard and yarn wraps. Pull the yarn through, pull it to the side opposite the cut ends, and tie the yarn tightly around the wrapped yarns with a knot. Cut the wrapped yarns on the opposite side from the tie.

Center the tied end of the pom-pom on the top of the head. Whip stitch the tied end of the pom-pom to the top of the head with a few stitches. To make curls, take each length of yarn, untwist the plies a bit, insert the tip of your needle between the plies, and pull the plies apart. After unplying all the yarn, distribute the hair around the head and trim the front yarn for bangs. Fluff up the hair.

Step 9. Face and Taking Flight

Because the fairy's face is small, I suggest using beads for the eyes and embroidery floss for the mouth. Or you can leave your fairy without facial features as I did.

To make your fairy fly, cut a length of fishing line, yarn, or ribbon about 18 inches long. Thread it onto the yarn needle and connect it to the body by entering the needle on one side of the wings and exiting the other. Tie the ends into an overhand knot.

May your Fiber Fairy bring you luck and joy!

Fig. 6a

Fig. 6b

Fig. 6c

PROJECT 9
Marias the Mermaid

THE PROJECTS

AS "EVERYONE KNOWS," most mermaids are named after a body of water. The Marias River runs through north central Montana until it joins the Missouri River. In 1806, the Lewis and Clark Expedition explored the Marias River, hoping it would lead up into Canada (it does not flow to Canada). Meriwether Lewis named the river after his cousin, Maria Wood, and we pronounce the river's name Mah-RYE-us.

As is fitting for a mermaid, Marias has a lovely, curvy hourglass figure.

> **Supplies Needed**
> - 40 yards green DK or light worsted knitting yarn
> - 32 yards pink DK or light worsted knitting yarn
> - 3 yards yellow fingering weight knitting yarn for her hair
> - 1 12-inch pipe cleaner
> - Black and red fingering weight yarn or embroidery floss for eyes and mouth
> - Stuffing
> - 1 3-inch-square piece of cardboard for hair pom-poms
>
> **Weave the squares as follows:**
> - 5 squares of green yarn
> - 4 squares of pink yarn

Step 1. Body and Tail

Body: Take 2 green squares and lay them on top of each other, matching the edges and corners. On one edge, stitch a ¼-inch seam. Open it into a rectangle. Repeat with 2 more green squares. You now have 2 rectangles made of 2 squares each.

Open and lay the rectangles on top of each other, with the right sides together. Stitch the seam along one long edge, starting with a ¼-inch seam, curving to a ½-inch seam at the center seam between the squares, curving out again to a ¼-inch seam at midpoint of the second square, and curving it back so you end the seam 1 inch away from the edge. Repeat this seam on the opposite long edge. (See Fig. 1a.) You will have a curvy, hourglass-shaped tube open on both ends. This is the body.

Turn the body right side out. The wider end of the tube, where you started with a ¼-inch seams, is the shoulders, and the narrow end with 1-inch seams on each side is the tail end. Stuff the body. Set aside.

Tail: Take another green square and fold it into a triangle. Measure ½ inch from the center of the folded edge toward the top point and make a ¼-inch-long tacking stitch parallel to the folded edge centered in the width to the triangle. To make a tacking stitch, insert the yarn needle threaded with green yarn from bottom to top, then insert the needle ¼ inch from the starting point, down through both layers, then up at the same spot you began the stitch, and knot the yarn. (See Fig. 1b.) Turn the triangle right side out, so the tack stitch line is on the inside of the tail now. Match the points and

Fig. 1a

Fig. 1b

Fig. 1c

57

looped edges and whip stitch the edges together through the loops. The tack stitch makes the tail curve up at the bottom center of the tail. (See Fig. 1c.)

Place the top point of the tail in the narrow opening on the body, so the body overlaps the tail's top point about ½ inch and the seam lines on the body match the outside edges of the tail. Slip stitch the body opening through the loops to the top point of the tail. Set the body aside.

Step 2. Arms and Shoulders

Take the pipe cleaner, and on each end, fold the ends back 1 inch so the pipe cleaner now measures 10 inches. Twist the folded ends to the longer piece. Caution: Simply cutting the pipe cleaner to 10 inches will likely result in the sharp wire ends of the pipe cleaner poking out through the fabric. Folding the pipe cleaner ends back prevents that from happening.

Arms: Take one of the pink squares and lay it on a flat surface. Place the pipe cleaner along the square's edge closest to you, so that the folded tip of the pipe cleaner is at the left-hand edge of the square. Roll the square tightly around the pipe cleaner. Slip stitch the looped edge of the square to the rolled portion along the long edge, and slip stitch across the short edge that will be the hand end through the loops. Repeat these steps with another pink square on the other folded-over end of the pipe cleaner. You now have a rolled pink square on each end of your pipe cleaner with the middle section of the pipe cleaner uncovered. These are the arms. (See Fig. 2a.)

Shoulders: Lay another pink square on a flat surface. This square will be the shoulders. Lay the arms on the shoulder square, so the arms are centered on the shoulder square and the seams on the arms are toward the back. Fold the shoulder square in half, so the uncovered portion of the pipe cleaner is now enclosed in the fold of the shoulder square and the edges of the shoulder square match. Turn both top corners of the shoulder square to the inside of the shoulder square, about ½ inch in each side. The folded edges should make a slope on each side. Pin the corners. Adjust the arms / pipe cleaner so that the edges of the shoulder slightly overlap the tops of the arms. On one side, slip stitch the looped edge of the shoulder to the arm around the top of the arm. Slip stitch the folds on the shoulder edge together at the top of the shoulder. Repeat for other arm / shoulder. Leave a 1-inch opening on the top of the shoulders between the folded corners for attaching the head. Stuff the shoulders. (See Fig. 2b.)

Place the shoulders on the top of the body, so the arms line up

Fig. 2c

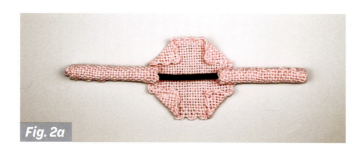
Fig. 2a

Fig. 2b

with the body side seams. Pin the edge of the top of the body to the shoulders and slip stitch with green yarn through the loops on the edge of the body to the shoulders all the way around the body. (See Fig. 2c.)

Step 3. Head

Take the remaining pink square and stitch a running stitch around the entire outside edge, ¼ inch from the edge, rounding the stitching line past the corners. Pull both ends of the yarn like a drawstring to gather the square into a bag, leaving a small opening for stuffing. Stuff the head firmly, then pull on the ends of the running stitch line to close the opening. Tie the ends of the drawstring with a knot and trim the ends close to the knot.

Fold the points on the gathered edge over to the center of the bottom of the head. Slip stitch these edges to the bottom of the head. Place the gathered end of the head into the opening in the shoulders, so the gathered end is at the back of the head, where the gathers will be hidden by the hair. To create a neck and secure the head to the body, slip stitch the shoulder edges through the loops to the bottom of the head, where the head and opening in the shoulders touch.

Step 4. Hair

Cut a piece of cardboard 3 inches square. The yellow yarn is used to make 5 pom-poms for the hair.

Wrap the yellow yarn around the cardboard 8 times, starting and ending on the same edge. Thread the yarn needle with a piece of yellow yarn; slip the yarn needle between the cardboard and yarn wraps. Pull the yarn through, leaving a short tail. Pull the yarn to the edge of the cardboard without the cut ends. Tie the yarn tightly around the wraps with a knot. Trim the tie ends close to the knot. Cut the yarn loops on the edge opposite the tie. You have 1 hair pom-pom. Make a total of 5 pom-poms for hair.

Place the first pom-pom with the tie centered on top of the head, so the hair frames the face. Stitch the center of the pom-pom to the head with yellow yarn. Place the next pom-pom behind the first, lining up the ties and stitching the pom-pom to the head. Continue placing pom-poms down the back of the head, lining up the ties so Marias has a "center part" in her hair.

Unply the yarn to create curly hair. Working one length of yarn at a time, untwist the yarn and insert the tip of your yarn needle between the plies. Pull the needle to the cut end of the yarn, unplying the yarn as it goes. Continue until you have unplied all the lengths of yarn.

Step 5. Face and Final Details

If you would like your mermaid to have a more defined waist, pinch the back of the body together between the waist curves on the sides to create a pleat / dart. Slip stitch the edges of the pleat together.

Using embroidery floss or fingering weight yarn, make 2 French knots for the eyes, wrapping the yarn only once around the needle. To stitch the mouth, do 2 backstitches, one for each side of the mouth, in a shallow "V" shape.

To help Marias sit, bend the body at the hipline and place her hands on her lap. Slip stitch the lower edges of the hands / arms to her lap.

Take her to a pond, lake, stream, or river, because every body of water should have a mermaid!

PROJECT 10
Polaris the Penguin

POLARIS THE PENGUIN is named for an unincorporated town located in the Pioneer Mountains of southwestern Montana. At one point in history, it was a booming mining town named for the Polaris Mine, where silver ore was extracted until 1922. Polaris the Penguin is modeled after the Adélie penguin species, which are the classic "tuxedo" penguins with a white chest / belly and black back, head, and wings. Very elegant birds!

Supplies Needed

64 yards black DK or light worsted knitting yarn

16 yards white DK or light worsted knitting yarn

16 yards rust DK weight or light worsted knitting yarn

Stuffing

Bright blue felt for eyes (template for eyes is in the appendix)

Blue sewing thread and needle for stitching on the eyes

Weave the squares as follows:

8 squares of black yarn
2 squares of white yarn
2 squares of rust yarn

Step 1. Body

Refer to "Large Tube" on page 22 for step-by-step photos of constructing the body.

Take 1 black and 1 white square and lay them on top of each other, matching the corners and edges. Stitch a ¼-inch seam along one edge. Open into a rectangle with the right side up. Take another black square and lay it right sides together on the white square in the rectangle, matching the outside end edges and corners. Stitch a ¼-inch seam on the outside end edge, joining the new black square to the white square. You now have a rectangle made up of 3 squares in this order—black/white/black. Set aside.

Make another black/white/black rectangle. The white squares will be the penguin's tummy, and the black squares the penguin's sides and back.

Lay the 2 rectangles on top of each other, with the right sides together, matching the long edges, seam lines, and corners. Stitch a ¼-inch seam along one long edge. Open. You now have a large rectangle of 6 squares: 2 black squares stacked on the left side, 2 white squares stacked in the middle, and 2 black squares stacked on the right side.

Lay the large rectangle on a flat surface, with the right side up. Fold the right-hand side over to the left side, so the stacks of black squares are now on top of each other, with right sides together. Match the corners, seam lines, and edges of the black squares. Stitch a ¼-inch seam across the outside end edge, joining all the black squares. You now have a tube 2 squares high by 3 squares around and open on both ends of the tube. Leave the tube with the wrong side out.

Take another black square and place it in the opening on one end of the tube, with the right sides together. Match 1 corner of the square with the seam line between two black squares. Pin the corner. Line up the opposite corner of the square with the center of the edge of the white square. These corner points should stick up about ¼ inch above the tube opening edge. Line up / pin the remaining corners to the center between the pinned corners. Match and pin the edges of the square to the edges of the tube between the pinned points. Stitch the square into the opening with a ¼-inch seam, rounding past the square's corners as you stitch the seam. This square is the bum of your penguin's body.

Turn the body right side out through the top opening of the tube. Stuff the body to your desired firmness. Stitch a running stitch ¼ inch from the tube edge around the tube opening, leaving about a 1-inch tail at the beginning. Now, pull both ends of the running stitch yarn like a drawstring to gather the edges of the tube until the opening is about the same size around as the seam line at the bottom of the body. Tie the ends of the drawstring in a knot and trim the yarn ends close to the knot. Add / subtract stuffing if needed. This is the head / shoulders end of the penguin's body.

Step 2. Head

Take another black square and fold it into a triangle. Whip stitch through the loops for 1 inch, starting at a corner on the folded edge of the triangle. Stuff the stitched corner. The stuffed corner is the penguin's beak. The rest of the square becomes the top / sides of his head.

Fig. 2

Place the open edges of the head / beak square over the shoulders end of the body, so the beak is centered over the white belly squares. Match the corner opposite the beak to the back seam line between the black squares, so the point is just below the gathered shoulders. Pin the point. Place the side points of the square so they are at the seam lines between the white and black squares on each side of the body. Pin the points. Stuff the head, shaping it as you stuff. Now pin the looped edges of the head to the body, between the back and side points, so the edges lie smoothly against the body. Slip stitch the looped edges to the body, starting from one side of the beak, around shoulders, to the opposite side of the beak. Before you finish stitching under the beak, make any stuffing adjustments necessary to shape the head. Finish stitching the bottom of head to body under the beak. (See Fig. 2.) Set the body aside.

Step 3. Wings

(Refer to "Cone" on page 21 for step-by-step photos for shaping the wings.)

Take 1 black square and fold into a triangle. Stitch a ¼-inch seam from fold to point on one edge. Turn right side out. Make a cone shape by centering the seam line between the two points. The seam side is the underside of the wing. Slip stitch the underside flat looped edge of the opening to the other side of the cone. Repeat with another square.

The wide end of the cone with the looped edges is the shoulder end of the wing. The narrower point of the cone is the lower part of the wing.

Refer to the main project photo of Polaris for placement of the wings.

Place a wing on one side of the penguin, with the wing seam line side against the body and the point on the wide end matching the side seam line between the white chest square / black side square, so the back edge of the wing follows the sloped edge of the back of the head where you sewed the head to the body. Pin. Adjust until you are happy with the placement / angle of wing. Slip stitch the top edges of the wing through the loops to the body / shoulder. Repeat on the other side of body for the second wing. Set the body aside.

Fig. 4a

Fig. 4b

Step 4. Feet

Take one of your rust squares and fold it into a triangle. (See Fig. 4a.) Fold the triangle in half again, so the loop edges are all one side and the folded edges are together. Whip stitch the looped edges together and then slip stitch the folded edges together. (See Fig. 4b.)

Fig. 4c

Hold the triangle so the flat looped edge is the top edge. Fold the 2 corners on each side toward the backside of the triangle until the tips of the corners meet. The foot will look like "Home Plate" in baseball, so that's how I'll refer to this particular shape. Slip stitch the edges of the folded points to the bottom of the foot and stitch the looped edges together. (See Fig. 4c.)

Place the feet on the bottom of the body, with the flat / looped edge of the foot toward the penguin's back, the center point of Home Plate to the front of the body, and the side of the foot with the stitched-down points down. Slip stitch the flat edges of the feet to the body, so the pointed ends of the feet stick out in front of the belly. (Refer to the main project photo of Polaris for placement of the feet.)

Step 5. Face

The templates for Polaris's eyes are in the appendix. Cut 2 eyes out of bright blue felt. Place the eyes on each side of the face, centering the beak between the eyes so that the eyes are on the side of the head and centered above where the white belly / black back squares meet. Slip stitch the edges of the felt eyes to the head with sewing thread, or glue the eyes in place.

Take Polaris to the zoo to meet his cousins!

PROJECT 11
Olney the Owl

I LOVE OWLS. Olney the Owl—modeled on great horned owls—is named for Olney, Montana, an unincorporated area in far north-western Montana surrounded by the Kootnai National Forest and the Stillwater State Forest. The Stillwater Forest is the first designated state forest in Montana, established in 1925. An excellent home for owls!

Olney was inspired by great horned owls and great gray owls, which are both huge birds. Tiny Olney, on the other hand, is only 6-7 inches tall.

Supplies Needed

96 yards brown DK or light worsted knitting yarn

6 yards of white DK or light worsted knitting yarn

Stuffing

Black felt

Black sewing thread and needle

Weave the squares as follows:

12 squares of brown yarn

1 square of white yarn woven with brown yarn. (Wind the first three rounds on the loom with white yarn, then tie on brown yarn to weave the square. See the appendix for instructions for changing the weaving yarn color.)

Step 1. Body

Refer to "Large Tube" on page 22 for step-by-step photos for constructing the body.

Take 2 brown squares and lay them on top of each other, matching the corners and edges. Stitch a ¼-inch seam along one edge. Open it into a rectangle. Lay the rectangle on a flat surface with the right side up.

Place another brown square on top of one of the squares in the 2-square rectangle, matching the corners and edges. Stitch a ¼-inch seam on the outside end edge of the squares, so you have a rectangle of three brown squares across. Set aside.

Take another brown square and lay the white/brown square on top, matching the corners and edges. Stitch a ¼-inch seam on one edge. Open and lay the rectangle right side up on a flat surface. Place another brown square on top of the white/brown square, matching the

edges and corners. Stitch a ¼-inch seam on the outside end edge. You have a rectangle of 3 squares across: brown/white woven with brown/brown.

Lay the solid brown rectangle right side up on a flat surface. Lay the brown/white/brown rect-angle on top of the solid brown rectangle, so the right sides are together, matching the edges, corners, and seam lines. Stitch a ¼-inch seam along one long edge. Open. You have a large rectangle of 6 squares—2 squares high and 3 squares across. The white square is Olney's tummy, so the brown/white/brown rectangle is the bot-tom of the owl. The rectangle with three brown squares is the head.

Lay the large rectangle on a flat surface, with the right side up and each end 2 squares high. Take the right-hand outside edge and fold it over the rectangle to the left-hand outside edge, so the right sides are together. Pin the two square outside end edges together, matching the corners and center seam. Stitch a ¼-inch seam along this edge. You now have a tube that is 2 squares high and 3 squares around, and the wrong-side seam edges are on the outside of the tube. Leave the tube wrong side out.

Take another brown square and place it in the end of the tube with the white square. Match one point of the square to the seam line between the 2 brown squares. Pin. Now match the opposite corner of the square to the center of the white/brown square on the opposite side of the tube. Pin. The square corner points should be about ¼ inch above the edges of the tube. Line up the remaining corners of the square to the center between the two pinned points, and pin with the points about ¼ inch above the tube edge. Match the edges of the square with the edges of the tube opening between the pinned points, easing and pinning as you go. Stitch the square to the opening of the tube with a ¼-inch seam, rounding the seam past the corners, all the way around the edge of the tube. This end is the owl's bum.

Turn the body right side out through the tube opening. Stuff the body firmly. Stitch a running stitch around the open end, leaving a short tail at the beginning and end of the stitching line. Pull on the yarn

Fig. 1

ends like a drawstring to gather the edges of the tube until the top edge is about the same size around as the bottom seam line of the tube. The opening will not be completely closed. Tie the gathering yarn in a knot and trim the yarn ends close to knot. You now have the owl's body. (See Fig. 1.) Set the body aside.

Step 2. Head

Take another brown square. Fold into triangle, and on one corner by the fold, whip stitch through the loops from the fold to ¾ inch from the fold. Stuff the point you just stitched. This is the owl's beak.

Fig. 2a

Fig. 2b

Place the square over the top of the body, so the beak is centered over the white tummy square about ½ inch above the top seam line of the white square. (See Fig. 2a.) Pin. On the back of the head, match the point opposite the beak to the seam line on the back of the head. (See Fig. 2b.) Pin.

The two remaining points will stick out on each side of the head. These are the ears. Pin the front edge of the square on each side by the ear points that stick out, making sure the edges of the square lie flat on the gathered end of the body. Slip stitch the edges of the head square through the loops from one ear, down to the beak, then up the other side to the ear. Knot the yarn. On the back of the head, slip stitch through the loops the edges from ear to ear around the back middle point pinned to the body. Set the body aside. The ears remain open flaps on each side of the head.

Step 3. Wings

(Refer to "Cone" on page 21 for step-by-step photos for shaping the wings.)

Take one brown square and fold it into a triangle. Whip stitch the loops together on one edge from the fold to the center point of the triangle. Open it into a cone shape by centering the seam line between the sewn point and the opposite open end point. Fold the narrow sewn point down ½ inch to the seam side of the cone, then slip stitch the edges of folded point to wing. Repeat with 3 more brown squares for a total of 4 wings.

Place a wing on one side of the owl's body, matching the top folded edge of the wing to the body seam line between the head and the chest / tummy, with the front folded edge of the wing placed along the seam line for the white chest square. Pin the wing in place. Place a second wing on top of the first wing, with the front edge of the wing slightly forward toward the white tummy square. Pin. When you are happy with the wing placement, slip stitch the folded edges of the wings to the owl's body, leaving the wider wing tips open. Repeat for the wings on the other side of the body. (Refer to the main project photo of Olney for wing placement on the body.)

Step 4. Tail

Take the remaining brown square and fold one point down 1 inch. (See Fig. 4a.) Pin. Fold the looped edges on each side of the folded-down point so that the looped

Fig. 4a

Fig. 4b

edges meet in the center. Slip stitch the edges together through the loops and then slip stitch the folded edges together across the top. (See Fig. 4b.)

Center the seam side of the tail on the body back seam, placing the tail so the outside edges of the bottom point line up with the bottom of the body and the tail tip extends a little past the bottom of the body. Slip stitch the edges of the tail to the body, leaving the bottom point of the tail open.

Step 5. Face

The templates for the owl's eyes are in the appendix. Use this pattern to cut 2 eyes out of black felt. Place the eyes on the face, with the bottom of each eye even with the top of the beak and the inner edge of the eye lined up with the outside edge of the beak. Slip stitch the edges of the eyes to the owl's head, using black sewing thread. You can also glue the eyes to the head. Refer to the main project photo for face details.

To give the beak a little definition, using a little leftover brown yarn, use either a backstitch or split stitch to stitch a line across the upper edge of the beak.

Take Olney outside to visit his fellow feathered friends.

PROJECT 12
Laurel the Lion

THE PROJECTS

LAUREL THE LION is more abstract in design than some of the other Critters. African lions live on the plains of Africa, so it's appropriate that Laurel the Lion is named for Laurel, Montana, located on the prairies of central Montana.

> ### Supplies Needed
> - 128 yards light brown DK or light worsted knitting yarn
> - 25 yards dark brown DK or light worsted knitting yarn for mane and end of tail tuft
> - 2 yards black fingering weight yarn or embroidery floss for face *or* use the template in the appendix to use felt for the nose / eyes and embroidery floss for the mouth
> - Stuffing
> - 1-inch-wide x 4-inch-long piece of cardboard for making the mane and tail pom-poms
>
> ### Weave the squares as follows:
> 16 squares of light brown yarn

Step 1. Body

Refer to "Large Tube" on page 22 for step-by-step photos for constructing the body.

Laurel's body is a large tube shape like Harrison the Hedgehog but without the gathers on one end of the tube. Instead, both ends of Laurel's body are closed with squares, just like many other Critters. (See Fig. 1.)

Take 2 light brown squares and lay them on top of each other, matching the edges and corners. Stitch a ¼-inch seam along *one* edge. Open into a rectangle.

Take 2 more squares and stitch a ¼-inch seam on one edge. Open. Repeat with another two squares.

You now have 3 rectangles consisting of 2 squares each. Lay two rectangles on top of each other, with the right sides together, matching the corners, edges, and center seam lines. Stitch a ¼-inch seam along one long 2-square edge. Open. You have a large square. Take your last rectangle and lay it with the right sides together on one edge of the square, matching the edges / corners / seam lines, and stitch a ¼-inch seam on the long edge, joining the rectangle to the large square. You now have a large rectangle that is 2 squares across and 3 squares long.

Lay the large rectangle flat, with the right side up, so the 3

Fig. 1

69

square rows are top and bottom. Take the right-hand 2-square end of the rectangle and fold it over to meet the left-hand 2 square edge, so the right sides are together matching the edges / corners / seam lines. Pin. Stitch a ¼-inch seam along the outside 2 squares edge. You now have a tube open on both ends, 2 squares wide and 3 squares around. Leave the tube wrong side out.

Take another square and place it inside the opening on one end of the tube, matching one square point to a seam line on the tube. Pin the corner so the point sticks up about ¼ inch above the edge of the tube. This tube seam line will now be the center back of the lion's body. Pin the opposite corner of this square to the center of the square on the opposite side of the tube, with the point about ¼ inch above the tube edge. Pin. This side of the tube will be the lion's belly. Line up the remaining corners of the square between the two pinned points. These points will also extend ¼ inch above tube edge. Match the edges of the square to the edges of the tube between the pinned points, easing and pinning as you go. Stitch a ¼-inch seam around the entire edge of the square / tube, rounding the seam past the points. Don't worry too much if it isn't perfectly round. Take another square and repeat this process on the other open end of the tube, leaving a small opening between the beginning / end of the seam.

Turn the body right side out through the seam opening. Stuff

Fig. 3

the body firmly through the seam opening, so the ends bulge out just a bit for the bum and chest. Turn the edges of the seam opening under and slip stitch the seam opening closed. You now have a closed tube. Set the body aside.

Step 2. Head

This is the easiest head to create of all the Critters. Take 2 light brown squares and lay them on top of each other, matching the corners and edges. Stitch a ¼-inch seam around all edges, leaving a small opening between the beginning and end of the seam. Turn the head right side out through the seam opening and stuff it into a pillow shape. Turn the seam opening edges under and slip stitch the opening closed.

Pick one end of the body for the chest. Center the head on the chest so that the top of the head is about 1 inch above the level of the back of the body, with 2 corners of the square "pillow" at the top of the head and 2 corners at the bottom of the head. Slip stitch the back of the head to the chest on all edges that touch. Set aside.

Step 3. Legs

Take one of the light brown squares and fold it in half, matching the corners and edges. Starting at one corner of the long edge, stitch a ¼-inch seam along the long edge, around the next corner, and then across the short end to the fold. You now have a small rectangle open on one narrow edge. Turn the leg right side out through the open end. Stuff the leg so it makes a long pillow about ¾ inch high. Turn the edges of the opening under and slip stitch closed from the seam line to the folded edge. (See Fig. 3.) Make 3 more legs.

Front legs: Place one leg under the front of the body. so the leg sticks out about ½ inch farther than the front of the head and the seam edges of the leg are facing the centerline on the body. Slip stitch the edges of the leg to the bottom of the body where they touch. Repeat for the front leg on the other side. There should be about ¼ inch separating long edges of the legs on the underside of the body.

Back legs: Place a leg on one side of the lion's body, with the back end of the leg even with the seam line between the bum and the body, the seam line on the leg's long edge down, and the bottom edge of the leg at the bottom edge of the body. Slip stitch the leg edges to the body, starting about 1 inch from the bum end of the leg, around the narrow bum end of the leg, and stopping on the top edge of the leg about 1 inch from the bum. The end of the leg toward the front of the body is not stitched down to the body. Repeat for the other back leg on the other side of the body.

Step 4. Tail

Take the last 2 squares and lay them on top of each other, matching the corners / edges. Stitch a ¼-inch seam on one edge. Open it into a rectangle and lay the rectangle on a flat surface, with the wrong side up. Starting on the long edge closest to you, fold the edge over about ¼ inch and roll it to the top edge. Pin the looped edge to the rolled part of the tail and slip stitch through the loops the edge to the rolled part. Center one end of the tail at the seam line at the top of the lion's bum. Slip stitch through the loops the tail end to the body so the rest of the tail hangs free. (Refer to Laurel's main project photo for placement of the tail.)

Step 5. Mane and Tail Tufts

The mane and tail tufts are pom-poms pf the dark brown yarn, wound around a 1-inch-wide piece of cardboard or a ruler.

Mane: Make 12 pom-poms of 36 wraps each. Wind the yarn around the cardboard 36 times, starting and ending on the same edge of the cardboard. Thread your yarn needle with a bit of leftover light brown yarn, slip the needle between the yarn wraps and the cardboard, pull through the yarn, and pull the yarn to the edge of the cardboard without the cut ends of the wraps. Tie the yarn tightly around the wraps and trim the tie ends near the knot. Cut the wraps on the edge opposite the tie. Eleven of these large pom-poms are for the mane. The 12th large pom-pom is for the tail tuft.

Make 1 pom-pom of 20 wraps. This pom-pom will be the "bangs" at the top center of the head.

Placing the pom-poms: Take one of the large pom-poms and stitch the tied end of the pom-pom to the end of the tail. (Refer to Laurel's main project photo for placement of the pom-poms.)

The remaining pom-poms are for the mane. Center 1 pom-pom on the back of the head just above where the body and head meet, and stitch the tie end to the head. Place the next pom-pom above the first, but just below the seam at the top of the head.

Stitch one pom-pom behind each ear—the top corners on each side of head.

Stitch 2 pom-poms on each side of the head, with 1 pom-pom centered in the top half of the head and the second pom-pom centered on the bottom half of the head, placing both pom-poms just barely toward the back of the head from the side seam line of the head.

Stitch 1 pom-pom, matching the tie end to the seam line on each of the lower corners of the head and one pom-pom on the bottom middle of the head (chin). Fluff up all the pom-poms so they overlap and cover around the edges of the head.

Stitch the smaller 20 wraps pom-pom at the top center of the head, just a little forward from the seam for bangs.

Step 6. Face

You have two options for the face: You can use the eyes / nose template in the appendix and cut these out of black felt. You can either stitch the edges of the eyes / nose to the face with sewing thread or glue the pieces to the face. Embroider the mouth, using the black fingering weight yarn or embroidery floss using a split stitch. If you don't have black felt, you can embroider the facial features by using a split stitch to stitch the mouth and a satin stitch for the eyes and nose.

Laurel is ready to see the world!

PROJECT 13
Frazer the Frog

THE PROJECTS

FRAZER THE FROG is named for Frazer, a "census-designated place" of 420 people on the Fort Peck Indian Reservation in the northeastern corner of Montana. This area is also home to Fort Peck Lake, the fifth-largest artificial lake in the United States, created by a dam in the Missouri River. With the lake being so big and located within such a low human population area, you seldom see another person. Which means it's a perfect home for frogs and other aquatic critters!

For variety, you can make the underside of Frazer's head a different color.

Supplies Needed

- 88 yards green DK weight or light worsted knitting yarn
- 2 yards black fingering weight yarn or embroidery floss for face
- Stuffing
- You have the option of making the underside of Frazer's head a different color of yarn. (See below for yarn needs for contrasting body / belly squares.)

Weave the squares as follows:

- 11 squares of green yarn
- If you decide to use a contrasting color of yarn for the underside of the head: 10 squares of green (80 yards needed) and 1 square (8 yards) of contrasting / coordinating color.

Step 1. Body

Take 2 of the green squares and lay them on top of each other, matching the edges and corners. Stitch a ¼-inch seam along one edge. Open into a rectangle.

Take 2 more squares and lay them on top of each other, matching the edges and corners. Stitch a ¼-inch seam along one edge. Open into a rectangle

Lay one rectangle on a flat surface, with the right side up. Lay the second rectangle on top, with the seam lines down, so the right sides on the 2 rectangles are together, matching edges, corners, and seam line. Stitch a ¼-inch seam along one long edge. Open. You now have a large square made up of 4 small squares.

Lay the larger square you just made on a flat surface, with the right side up. Take another green square and lay it on top of one of the small squares, matching the corners and edges. Stitch a ¼-inch seam, starting at one edge point, along the edge to the middle point, and then along other edge to the point opposite the first point, joining the singe square to the large square. These 2 squares will form the head. (See Fig. 1a.)

Lay the big square so the new square you just added is on top. Fold the outside corners of the other three squares to the center of the large square (see Fig. 1b), so you have 3 triangles, one on each of the edges that are not the head. Match the edges of the triangle shapes to neighboring edges and stitch a ¼-inch seam from the folds out to the center point and back to the folded edge along all three triangles and the open end of the

Fig. 1a

73

Fig. 1b

head square, connecting these edges to the edge of neighboring triangle. On the final seam, leave a small opening on one edge to turn the body right side out. You will have a squarish shape with a point on one side, which is the head. Turn the body and head through the seam opening, making sure to push the point on the head out completely. Stuff the body to desired firmness, making sure the head is stuffed all the way to the point and the body / head is about 1½–2 inches thick, with the center of the body a little fuller than the edges. Turn the edges of the seam opening under and slip stitch the opening closed. This is the frog's body / head. The pointed end is the head / nose. The opposite flat end is the frog's bum. (See Fig. 1b.) Set aside.

Step 2. Legs

Take one square and fold it into a triangle. Stitch a ¼-inch seam tapering out to a ½-inch seam on one edge from the fold to the point. (See Fig. 2a.) Turn right side out and center the seam line with the point on the open end to make a cone shape. The wide end of the cone is the webbed foot. Repeat with 3 more squares so you have 4 web-footed legs total. Set 2 of the cones aside for the front legs. The other 2 cones will be the lower part of the back legs in the next step.

Upper section of back legs: Take another green square and fold it in half; mark the middle fold with a pin. Open the square and lay it with the pin side down. Take the bottom edge of the square and fold it toward the middle, matching the edges of the loops with the pin at the center of square. Fold the top edge of the square over to the pin, so the two looped edges meet at center. Fold it in half at the pin so the two folded edges are together and the looped edges folded to the center are enclosed inside the last fold. Slip stitch the folded edges together. This is the top of one back leg and is a narrow rectangle measuring about ¾ inch wide. (See Fig. 2b.) Repeat with another square to make the second upper leg.

Attaching the lower back legs to the upper back legs: Take one of the leg cone shapes you set aside, and place the narrow pointed end

Fig. 2a

Fig. 2b

Fig. 2c

of the cone on top of one narrow end of an upper leg rectangle, so the cone-shaped lower leg is at about a 45-degree angle with the upper leg. Make a tacking stitch through all layers and knot the thread on the backside of the upper leg. (See Fig. 2c.) Repeat with another cone-shaped lower leg and the other upper leg rectangle. You have 2 back legs.

Back leg placement: Place a back leg onto the side of the body, with the "knee" aimed toward the bum end of the body and the narrow flat edge of the upper leg ¾ inch away from the end of the body. Slip stitch the end of the upper leg to the side of the body around all edges that touch. Repeat for other back leg.

Front leg placement: Take one of the cone-shaped front legs and hold it with the seam line facing you. Fold the narrow point end down ½ inch, matching the point to the seam line on the backside of the leg. Slip stitch the point edges to backside of the leg. Repeat with the other front leg.

Place the front legs on each side of the front of the body, so the leg seamed side is toward the body and the front edge of the cone matches the head seam line on the body. This puts the front legs at a slight forward angle. Slip stitch the top of the leg to the body wherever they touch.

You are done! Frazer makes a really fun tossing toy!

THE PROJECTS

75

PROJECT 14
Dagmar the Dragon

DAGMAR THE DRAGON is the mythical, magical namesake of Dagmar, an unincorporated community established in 1906 by Danish immigrants in northeastern Montana. Many cultures have legends of dragons, but the winged dragon legends emerged in Europe during the Middle Ages. So naming Dagmar after a Montana town founded by Danish immigrants feels perfect.

Dagmar was first envisioned at The National Needlearts Association's 2014 wholesale show. An attendee's daughter showed me a picture of a dragon she had knitted, and I knew I had to figure out how to make little squares into a dragon.

Supplies Needed
- 96 yards green DK knitting yarn
- 16 yards magenta DK or light worsted knitting yarn
- 1 12-inch pipe cleaner
- 2 yards black fingering weight yarn or embroidery floss
- Stuffing

Weave the squares as follows:
- 12 squares of green yarn
- 2 squares of magenta yarn

Step 1. Body

Take 2 green squares and lay them on top of each other, matching the edges and corners. Stitch a ¼-inch seam along one edge. Open into a rectangle.

Take 2 more squares and lay them on top of each other, matching the edges and corners. Stitch a ¼-inch seam along one edge. Open into a rectangle.

Lay one rectangle on a flat surface, with the right side up. Lay the second rectangle on top, with the right side down, so the right sides of the rectangles are together. Match the edges, corners, and seam lines. Stitch a ¼-inch seam along one long edge. Open. You now have a large square made up of 4 small squares. Lay the large square flat, with the right side up.

Take another small square and lay it on top of one of the squares, matching the corners and edges. Stitch a ¼-inch seam along the 2 outside edges and around the corner between the two edges. (See Fig. 1a.) This square will help form the neck / shoulders. Do not turn this square at this point.

Fold the outside corners of the other three squares to the center of the large square, so you have 3 triangles, one on each of the edges that are not the neck / shoulders. Match the edges of the triangles to neighboring edges and stitch a ¼-inch seam from the folds out to the center point and back to the fold edge along all three triangles and the open point on the square you added in the last step, connecting each edge of a triangle to its neighboring edge. On the final seam, leave a small opening on one edge to turn the body right side out. You will have a square shape with a point on one side, which is the base of the neck / shoulders. (See Fig. 1b.) Turn the body through the seam opening, fully pushing the point on the neck

Fig. 1a

Fig. 1b

77

end out. Stuff the body firmly, making sure the neck is stuffed all the way to the point at the top of the neck and the body is nicely rounded, with a flatter bottom side opposite the neck end of the body. Turn the edges of the seam under the opening and slip stitch the opening closed. This is the dragon's body. Set the body aside.

Step 2. Neck

Take a green square and fold it into a triangle. Stitch a ¼-inch seam from the fold to the center point. Turn right side out. You now have a cone shape that has a closed point on one end and is open on the opposite end. Stuff the stitched point firmly until the cone is about half full. Place the large opening of the cone on the body over the point that is the shoulders / base of the neck. (See Fig. 3.) Match the seam in the neck with the center front of the body and center the point on the neck opening on the back of the body. Pin the edges of the neck to the body, adjusting and adding stuffing so the wide end of the neck is evenly stuffed between the top of the neck base / shoulders of the body and the neck piece you just added. Slip stitch through the loops around the base of the neck to the shoulders on the body.

Step 3. Tail

Take another green square and fold it into triangle. Stitch a ¼-inch seam from the fold to the top corner. Turn right side out. Stuff the triangle firmly into a cone shape from the tip to even with the edge of the opening. Place the tail on the back of the body, with the edges of the open end of the tail lined up with the seam lines on the lower part of the body; the seamed edge of the tail will be near the flat bottom of the body. Pin and slip stitch through the loops the edges of the tail to the back of the body. (See Fig. 3.) Set the body aside.

Step 4. Head

Take another green square, fold it into triangle, and starting 1 inch away from the fold, stitch a ¼-inch seam up one side, around the point, and then down the other edge, stopping seam 1 inch away from the fold. (See Fig. 4a.) The openings on each end of the seam are the ears.

Turn the head right side out through one of the ear openings and stuff the stitched point firmly. With the head facing you, insert your thumb in one ear opening and pointer finger in the other ear opening. Pinch the ears together so the tips of the ears meet over the

Fig. 4a

top of the head. (See Fig. 4b.) Hold the ears firmly and poke your finger against the bottom of the head to push the stuffing and bottom fabric up, making a dent on the bottom side of the head. At the base of one ear, insert your needle through the head, out at the base of the other ear, and back again a couple of times. Knot the stitching yarn and cut the yarn next to the knot.

Fig. 4b

Position the head on top of the neck, fitting the tip of the neck into the dent you made on the underside of the head. Slip stitch the bottom of the head to the top of the neck.

Step 5. Arms

Fold a green square into a triangle, then fold this triangle in half to make a smaller triangle, with all the looped edges on top of each other and the folded edges on top of each other. Fold it in half again, matching the looped edges and folded edges. Slip stitch the looped

Fig. 3

edges together. Then slip stitch the folded edges together. Repeat these steps with another green square for the second arm.

Step 6. Legs

(Refer to "Basic Legs" on page 19 for step-by-step photos for constructing the legs.)

Fold a green square in half and stitch a ¼-inch seam on the long edge and then across one short edge. Turn right side out through the opening at the end. Stuff the leg and slip stitch the opening closed from the seam line out. With the long seam side of the leg facing away from you, pinch the bottom end of the leg to make a foot about 1 inch long. At the fold, do a tacking stitch a couple of times through all the layers and stuffing. This is one leg. Repeat the steps with another green square for the second leg.

Attaching the arms: Place the arms on each side of the body, with the stitched looped edges toward the back of the body and the stitched folded-edge faces down the body. The top edge of arm should be slightly higher than the seam line at the base of the neck. Slip stitch the base of the arm to the body, where they touch. Repeat the steps for the other arm.

Attaching the legs: Place a leg on one side of the body, so the bottom of the foot is about even with the bottom of the body, and the top of the leg slants toward the back of the body. Slip stitch the top edges of the leg to the body where they touch. Repeat with the second leg on other side of the body.

Step 7. Wings

Lay the two magenta squares next to each other on a flat surface as diamond shapes, with the inside corners on the squares overlapping by ½ inch. You have two diamond shapes connected in the middle. Slip stitch the overlapping corner points together. Lay the full length of the pipe cleaner across the diamonds, so it goes across the stitched center points and the outside points on each side. Turn the ends of the pipe cleaner back, so the pipe cleaner length is the same as the width of the wings from outside point to outside point of the diamond shapes. (See Fig. 7a.) Twist the folded-over ends around the pipe cleaner, so sharp ends won't stick out of the wings. Fold the diamonds in half over the pipe cleaner, so the pipe cleaner is enclosed in the wings at the fold and the looped edges of the squares are on top of each other. You now have 2 triangle shapes connected in the middle. (See Fig. 7b.) With magenta yarn, stitch a running stitch across the wings just below the pipe cleaner to make a "sleeve" to hold the pipe cleaner in place. Now whip stitch through the loops on the looped edges to join the wing edges.

Place the center of the wings on the back of the dragon about even with the tops of the arms. Slip stitch the edges of the wings to the back of the dragon where they touch.

Step 8. Face

Use the black fingering weight yarn or black embroidery floss to make 2 French knots on each side of the head for eyes. Use an outline or split stitch for the mouth.

Your dragon is ready for adventures!

Fig. 7a

Fig. 7b

PROJECT 15
Kiowa the Kangaroo

THE PROJECTS

KIOWA THE KANGAROO is named for an area on the eastern side of Glacier National Park, population four people (seriously, that is not a typo), near the town of Browning on the Blackfeet Indian Reservation. While kangaroos are not native to North America, this area of Montana is very similar in geography to the plains / mountains in Australia that support kangaroos. Kiowa is similar in construction to Dagmar the Dragon, so the "how to" photos will look familiar.

Supplies Needed
120 yards brown DK knitting yarn
2 yards black fingering weight yarn or embroidery floss for face
Stuffing

Weave the squares as follows:
15 squares of brown yarn

Step 1. Body

Take 2 of the squares and lay them on top of each other, matching the edges and corners. Stitch a ¼-inch seam along one edge. Open it into a rectangle.

Take 2 more squares and lay them on top of each other, matching the edges and corners. Stitch a ¼-inch seam along one edge. Open into a rectangle.

Lay one rectangle on a flat surface, with the right side up. Lay the second rectangle on top, with the right side down, so the right sides of the rectangles are together. Match and pin the seam lines, edges, and corners of the rectangles on one long edge. Stitch a ¼-inch seam along pinned long edge. Open. You now have a large square made up of 4 small squares.

Take another square and lay it on top of one of the squares in the large square, with the right sides together, matching the corners and edges. Stitch a ¼-inch seam along the 2 outside edges and around the corner between the two edges. (See Fig. 1a.) This square will help form the neck / shoulders. Do not turn this square yet.

Fold the outside corners of the other three squares to the center of the large square, so you have 3 triangles, one on each of the edges that are NOT the neck / shoulders. Match the edges of the triangles / square to neighboring edges and stitch ¼-inch seams from the folds out to the center point and back to the fold edge along all three triangles and the square, connecting those edges to the neighboring edges. On the final seam, leave a small opening on one edge to turn the body right side out. You will have a square with a point on one side, which is the base of the neck / shoulders. (See Fig. 1b.) Turn the body right side out through the seam opening, pushing the point on the neck end out. Stuff the body firmly, making sure the neck base is stuffed all the way to the point at top of neck and the body is nicely rounded with a slightly flattened bottom. Slip stitch the seam opening closed. This is the kangaroo's body / bottom part of the neck. Set aside.

Step 2. Neck

Take a square and fold it into a triangle. Stitch a ¼-inch seam on one edge from the fold to the top /

Fig. 1a

Fig. 1b

81

center corner. Turn it right side out and stuff. You now have a cone shape, with the narrow end at the top of the neck and the wider / open end that will help form the shoulders. Stuff the stitched point firmly until the cone is about half full. Place the opening of the cone over the top point on the body—the shoulders / base of neck. Center the seam line on the neck with the center front of the body, and center the point on the cone opening on the back of the body. Pin the neck edges to the body, adjusting the stuffing as needed around the neck / shoulders while making sure there is plenty of stuffing between the inner point on the body and the neck. Slip stitch the cone neck edges through the loops to the shoulders on the body.

Step 3. Tail

Take another square and fold it into a triangle. Stitch a ¼-inch seam on one edge from the fold to the center corner. Turn it right side out. You now have a cone shape. The narrow stitched point is the end of the tail, and the open end is attached to the body. Stuff the closed point of the cone firmly all the way to the open end of the cone. Place the tail on the lower back of the body, so the tail seam line is down and the open end point matches the seam line intersection on the back of the body. Pin the edges and slip stitch through the loops at the edges of the tail to the back of the body. (See Fig. 3.) Set the body aside.

Step 4. Mum's Head

Take another square, fold into a triangle, and starting 1 inch away from the fold, stitch a ¼-inch seam up one side, around the point, and down the next side, stopping 1 inch away from the other end of the fold. (See Fig. 4a.)

Fig. 4a

The openings / flaps on each side of the head become the kangaroo's ears. Turn the head right side out through one of the ear openings and stuff the stitched point firmly. With the head facing you, insert your thumb in one ear opening and a finger in the other ear opening. Pinch the ears together so the tips of the ears meet over the top of the head. (See Fig. 4b.) Hold ears firmly and poke your finger against the bottom of the head by the ears to push the stuffing and bottom fabric up into the head, making a dent. At the base of one ear, insert your needle through the head, out at the base of other ear, and back again a couple of times. Knot the stitching yarn and trim ends close to the knot.

Fig. 4b

Position Mum's head on top of the neck, fitting the top of the neck into the dent you made on the underside of the head. Slip stitch the edges of the dent on the underside of the head to the top of the neck so she's looking down toward her Baby in the pouch.

Refer to the main project photo for placement of the arms, legs, and pouch.

Step 5. Arms

Fold a square in half and roll tightly from one narrow end. Slip stitch the looped edge to the rolled part of the arm. The end with the looped edges together is the shoulder end. Slip stitch together the loops on the shoulder end. The end of the arm with the rolled-up fold will be the paw, and you can pull the folds out a little bit to make a pointy shape on

Fig. 3

the end for the paw. Repeat with another square for the other arm.

Step 6. Legs

(Refer to "Basic Legs" on page 19 for step-by-step photos for constructing the legs.)

Fold a square in half and stitch a ¼-inch seam on the long edge and then across one short edge. Turn right side out through the opening at the end. Stuff leg and slip stitch the opening closed from the seam out. With the long seam edge facing away from you, pinch the bottom end of the leg to make a foot that is about 1½ inches long. At the fold, do a tacking stitch a couple of times through all layers / stuffing, knotting the yarn on the bottom of the foot. Do another tacking stitch through the foot about a ¼ inch back from the toe to flatten the foot. This is one leg. Repeat with another square for second leg.

Attaching the arms: Place the arms on each side of the body, with the stitched-together looped edges toward the back of the body and the stitched seam line facing down the body. The top edge of the arm should be placed about at the seam line at the base of the neck. Slip stitch the base of the arm to the body where the edges touch. Repeat for the other arm.

Attaching the legs: Place a leg on one side of the body, so the bottom of the foot is about even with the bottom of the body and the leg slants toward the back. Slip stitch the top edges of the leg to the body where they touch. Repeat on the other side of the body.

Step 7. Pouch

Take a square and fold into a triangle. Whip stitch the loops together around both sides of the triangle from one end of the fold to the other end of the fold. Place the pouch so the center point is low on Mum's belly, the side points line up with the body seams on each side of the body, and the front of the pouch bulges out a bit. Adjust until you like the placement. Pin and slip stitch the looped edges of the pouch to the body. Set the body aside.

Step 8. Baby

Baby's head: Take a square and fold into a triangle, then fold triangle in half so looped edges are together and folded edges are together. Slip stitch the folded edges together. On the looped-edges side, slip stitch the loops together for ½ inch, centered between the end points of that edge of the triangle. This stitched edge is the top of the Baby's head, and the unstitched openings on each side of the looped edge are

Fig. 8

the ears. (See Fig. 8.) Pinch the 2 ears together over the ½ inch you stitched in the center of the looped edge, and stitch the bases of the ears together like you did for Mum's ears. Do not add stuffing to Baby's head since the fabric acts as stuffing. Push your finger into the underside of Baby's head to make a dent like you did with Mum's head.

Baby's body: Take the last square, fold it in half, and roll tightly from a narrow end. Slip stitch the end looped edge to the roll. Place one end of body in the dent on the underside of Baby's head. Slip stitch the bottom of the head to the top of the body around the top of the body.

Place the Baby into the pouch, so only the head shows. Do a couple of stitches at the base of the head / top of body to attach the Baby to the front of the pouch.

Faces: Both Mum's and Baby's faces are stitched with black fingering weight yarn or embroidery floss. The eyes are French knots on each side of the head, and the mouths are split stitch or outline stitch.

That's it! You have a kangaroo Mum with her joey ready to explore!

PROJECT 16
Tarkio the T-Rex

DID YOU KNOW that Montana was a prime stomping (pun intended) ground for Tyrannosaurus Rex dinosaurs? In fact, the first T-Rex skeleton ever found by humans was unearthed in 1902 in Hell Creek, Montana. Tarkio the T-Rex is named for an unincorporated area in Mineral County. As far as I know, no dinosaur fossils have been found in Tarkio. Yet.

Tarkio is similar in construction to Dagmar the Dragon and Kiowa the Kangaroo.

Supplies Needed

138 yards green DK weight knitting yarn

46 yards solid orange or variegated orange/yellow DK knitting yarn

2 yards black fingering weight yarn or embroidery floss

Stuffing

Weave the squares as follows:

23 squares of green yarn woven with the orange/variegated yarn. You will wind the green yarn onto the loom for the first 3 rounds and then tie on the orange/variegated yarn to weave the squares. See the appendix for instructions / photos of connecting a different color of yarn for weaving.

Step 1. Body

Take 2 squares and lay them on top of each other, matching the corners and edges. Stitch a ¼-inch seam along one edge. Open. You now have rectangle #1 made up of 2 squares. Repeat to make two more rectangles of 2 squares each. These are rectangles #2 and #4. You have a total of 3 rectangles made up of 2 squares each.

Lay 2 more squares on top of each other and stitch a ¼-inch seam on one edge. Open into rectangle and place another square on one outside end, matching the corners / edges. Stitch a ¼-inch seam on the outside end edges. Open into a rectangle consisting of 3 squares. This is rectangle #3.

Take rectangles #1 and #2 (of 2 squares each) and lay them right sides together on top of each other, matching edges, corners, and seam lines. Stitch a ¼-inch seam on one long edge. Open. You now have a square consisting of 4 small squares.

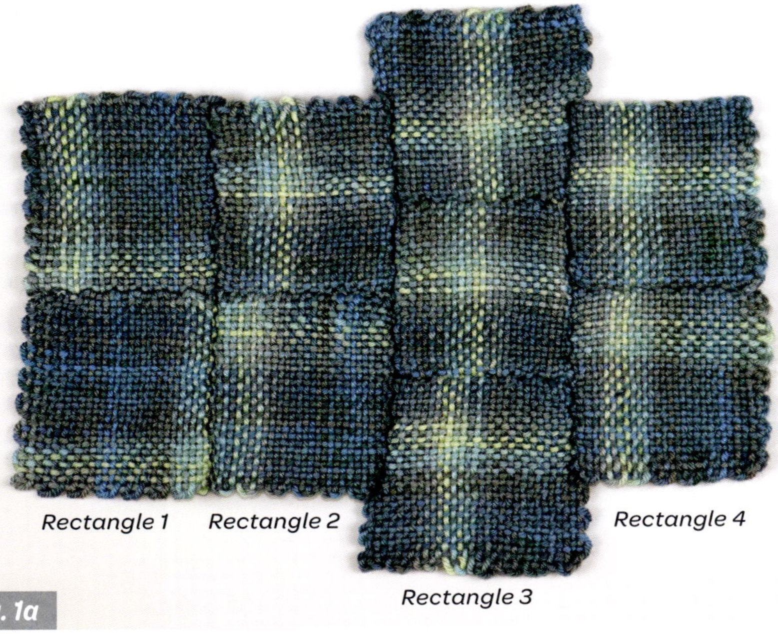

Rectangle 1   Rectangle 2   Rectangle 4

Rectangle 3

Fig. 1a

Fig. 1b

Take rectangle #3 (consisting of 3 squares) and lay it on top of one of the edges of the square, with the right sides together, matching the edges and matching the seam line of the large square, with the center of the middle square on rectangle #3. Stitch a ¼-inch seam along this edge. Open. You will now have a capital "T" shape, with the square of 2 rectangles as the leg of the "T" and rectangle #3 as the crossbar of the "T."

Take rectangle #4, composed of 2 squares, and lay it right sides together on top of the 3-square rectangle, matching the edges, and center the seam line on rectangle #4, with the center of the middle square of rectangle #3. Stitch a ¼-inch seam along the edge. You now have a shape resembling a lowercase "t." (See Fig. 1a.)

Fold the body rectangles with right sides together, matching the edges and corners, using the center seam lines on the 3 2-square rectangles as your folding line. The folded rectangle #4 is the neck. The folded section with rectangle #3, composed of 3 squares, is the belly. The section with rectangles #1 and #2 together is the tail end of the body.

Start the belly seam from the neck end of the body, and start the seam 1 inch away from the edge. As you stitch, taper the seam down so it's ¼ inch at the seam line between the neck and belly. Round the seam down past the first corner on the belly squares, so at the middle of the belly, the seam is about ¼ inch from the edge. Now round the seam up past the opposite corner of the belly, so the seam is ¼ inch when you reach the seam line between the belly rectangle and the start of the tail. Continue the seam onto the tail end, tapering from a ¼-inch seam for the belly to 1 inch away from the edges at the seam between rectangles #1 and #2 on the tail end. Finish the seam 1 inch from the belly edge. (See Fig. 1b.) Turn right side out through the neck end opening and stuff the body firmly. Set the body aside.

Finishing the tail: Take 1 square and fold it into a triangle, matching the edges and the top point. Stitch a ¼-inch seam along 1 edge from fold to point. Turn right side out and stuff the tail from the tip to all the way to the large opening to make a stuffed cone shape. This is the tip of the tail. (See Fig. 1c.)

Place the opening of the tail tip onto the opening on the longer tail end of the body, so the point on the open end of the tail is centered on the back of the body tail section and the tail tip seam matches the belly seam line on the belly side of the body. Pin, adjust the stuffing as necessary, and slip stitch through the loops the edges of the tail tip opening to the body. Set the body aside.

Step 2. Head

Take 2 squares and lay them on top of each other, matching the edges and corners. Stitch a ¼-inch seam

Fig. 1c

Fig. 2a

on one edge and a ¼-inch seam on opposite edge, so you have a tube open on each end. Turn right side out and stuff firmly, shaping into a rounded rectangle-like shape. (See Fig. 2a.) The seam lines will be on the sides of the head.

On one end, turn the seam line edges of the tube so the edges meet at the center of the opening. This fold will be about ½ inch on

Fig. 2b

Fig. 2c

each side. Turn the lower flap of the opening up, and slip stitch the edges of the flap to the folded-in fabric from the sides of the head. (See Figs. 2b and 2c.)

Fold down the top flap of the opening and slip stitch the bottom edge of the top flap to the lower flap, leaving the folds / bulges on each side open to make nostrils. (See Fig. 2d.)

On the back open side of the head, stitch a running stitch ¼ inch

Fig. 2d

away from the edge around the opening, leaving a short starting and ending tail. Pull stitching yarn by the tails like a drawstring until the opening is closed completely.

Fig. 2e

Tie gathering yarn with a knot and trim yarn ends close to knot. Place the head on the opening on the neck end of the body and slip stitch the edges of neck to bottom of the head. (See Fig. 2e.) Make sure the nostrils are on the top side of the head before stitching the head to the neck!

Now you will be covering the back of the head, so you have a nice smooth line from the back to the top of the head. Take another square and place one point of the square at the center of the head, about 2½ inches back from the front of the head. Pin the point. Place the opposite point of the square to match the back seam line on the neck section of the body. Pin. Place stuffing under the square so the square lies smoothly down the back of the head to the back. Pin the remaining points to sides of the neck and slip stitch through the loops the neck cover to the body around all edges of the square. (See Fig. 2f.) Set the body aside.

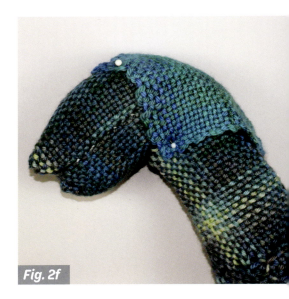

Fig. 2f

87

Step 3. Upper Legs

Fold a square into a triangle, then fold the triangle in half so the looped edges match. Now fold this smaller triangle in half, again matching the looped edges. The looped edges should be stacked up together, and the folded edges should be stacked up together. Slip stitch the looped edges together and then slip stitch the folded edges together. Repeat with another square for the other upper leg.

Place the upper legs on each side of the body, so the stitched-loops edge is toward the back and the stitched-folds edge is down. Place the bottom tip of the triangle to match the seam line between the neck and belly on the body. Slip stitch the edges of arms to the body wherever they touch. (Refer to the main project photo of Tarkio to see the placement of the upper and lower legs.)

Step 4. Lower Legs

Each lower leg takes 4 squares. Lay two squares on top of each other, matching the corners and edges. Stitch a ¼-inch seam on one edge. Open into rectangle. Repeat with 2 more squares. You have 2 rectangles of 2 squares each. Lay the rectangles on top of each other, with right sides together, matching edges, seam lines, and corners. Stitch a ¼-inch seam along one long edge.

Open into large square and lay flat on a surface, with right side up. Fold the large square into a large triangle, with right sides together and edges / corners matching. On one edge, stitch seam from the fold, starting with a ¼-inch seam at the point and gradually increasing to 1-inch seam at seam line between the squares, then gradually decrease the seam to ¼ inch at the point of the large triangle. (See Fig. 4.) You will have a large cone shape. Turn right side out and stuff firmly all the way from the point to the top opening. Repeat these steps for the second lower leg.

Place a lower leg on one side of the body, so the leg opening is against the body and the leg seam matches the seam line between the tail squares and the belly squares. The top point of the leg opening should be centered in the belly squares, with the tip about ½ inch above the seam line on the side. Pin the edges of the leg to the body and add extra stuffing to the top portion of the leg, if necessary, to give Tarkio nice muscular thighs. Slip stitch the leg-opening edges through the loops to the body. Repeat for second leg. (Refer to the main project photo of Tarkio for placement.)

Feet: Hold Tarkio so you are looking at his front. Pinch the bottom point of a lower leg and fold it up 1½ inches. Slip stitch the edges of the fold to each other to create an ankle. Repeat for other lower leg, making sure the lower legs are the same length.

Face: Using the black fingering weight yarn or embroidery floss, make 2 large French knots for the eyes, wrapping the yarn around your needle about 5 times. Using a split stitch or outline stitch, stitch his mouth.

Introduce Tarkio to the budding paleontologist at your house!

Fig. 4

THE PROJECTS

PROJECT 17
Clancy the Chameleon

THE PROJECTS

I THINK CHAMELEONS are the coolest of all the reptiles. Their ability to change color, the way their eyes move independently, and their feet, which are perfect for gripping branches, are so distinctive. Clancy the Chameleon is named for the unincorporated town of Clancy, Montana, established in 1873 as a gold-mining town and named for a prospector, William Clancy.

To personalize Clancy, you can give him a cool-looking crest on his head.

Supplies Needed
112 yards multicolored DK or light worsted knitting yarn
2 yards black fingering weight yarn or embroidery floss for face
Stuffing
2 12-inch-long pipe cleaners

Weave the squares as follows:
14 squares of multicolored DK or light worsted knitting yarn

Step 1. Body

Take 2 squares and lay them on top of each other, matching edges / corners. Stitch a ¼-inch seam on one edge. Open. You have a rectangle composed of 2 squares. Set aside.

Take 2 more squares, lay them on top of each other, matching the edges / corners, and stitch a ¼-inch seam on one side. Open and place on flat surface, with right side up. Lay another square on top of the square on the right-hand side of the rectangle, matching the outside end edge / corners. Stitch a ¼-inch seam on this outside end edge. Open. You now have a long rectangle composed of 3 squares.

Lay the long 3-square rectangle on a flat surface, with the right side up. Lay the 2-square rectangle on top of the 2 right hand squares of the long rectangle, with right sides together matching edges, corner, and seam lines. Stitch a ¼-inch seam to join the rectangles on long edge. Open. You now have a stairstep design with the 2-square rectangle above the 3-square rectangle.

Lay the stairstep rectangles on flat surface, with right side up, with the 2-square rectangle at the top of the stair-step. Take another square and place it on the lower right-hand square of the large 3-square rectangle, matching the corners / edges. Stitch a ¼-inch seam, attaching the bottom edge of this last square to the bottom edge of the far right square of the 3-square rectangle. (See Fig. 1a for how the squares should look from the right side when all pieces are sewn together.)

Lay the body right side up on a flat surface, as shown in Fig. 1a. Take the single square at the bottom and fold it over to the left, so the last square in the 3-square rectangle becomes a triangle and the right side of the single square of the bottom row and the middle square of the 3-square rectangle are together. (See Fig. 1b.) Stitch a ¼-inch seam connecting the bottom

Fig. 1a

Fig. 1b

91

Fig. 1c

Fig. 1d

edge of the middle square with the left-hand edge of the single square.

Now fold the top rectangle over the long middle rectangle, so the top edge of the left-hand square of the 2-square rectangle matches the outside end edge of the first square in the long 3-square rectangle and the right sides of fabric are together. (See Fig. 1c.) Stitch a ¼-inch seam connecting those two edges.

Place the fabric on a flat surface, so the square at the top looks like a diamond shape. Now take the point at the top of the diamond and fold the point down so the edges/point match the edges and seam line point of the squares on each side of the bottom of the diamond. Stitch a ¼-inch seam on both edges. You now have a tube where all the squares are on bias and the 2 ends are open. (See Fig. 1d.)

Turn body right side out through one of the openings. Stuff the body firmly. Once stuffed, the body will be a shallow "S" shape, with openings on both ends. (See Fig. 1e.) The end that turns upward is for the head. The end that turns downward is the tail end. Set the body aside.

Step 2. Tail

Take one square and lay it on a flat surface. Starting on one side, roll the edge of the square into a cone shape, with a point being the narrow end of the cone and the opposite point being the wider end about 1½ inches across. Slip stitch the looped edge to the rolled portion of the cone. This is the tail tip. (See Fig. 2a.) I have purposely made the tail sections with different-colored yarns so how to put together the tail pieces is easier to see in the photo. For your chameleon, these squares should be the same yarn as the rest of the body.

Take another square and fold it into a triangle. Stitch a ¼-inch seam from the point to 1 inch away from the folded edge on one side of the triangle. (See Fig. 2b.) Turn right side out. This is the tail base.

Stuff both sections of the tail. Now take the rolled cone you made for the tail tip and insert the open end of tail tip into the 1-inch opening in the seam of the tail base, matching the point on the tail base to the end of the seam of the tail tip. Match the seam line on the tail base to the point on the opening of the tail tip, and whip stitch through the loops to connect the tail sections together. Adjust the tail stuffing if necessary.

The tail end of the body turns downward. Line up the open end of the tail base to the back end of the body, matching the seam line on the tail base to the seam line on the back of the body. Match

Fig. 2b

Fig. 1e

Fig. 2a

THE PROJECTS

Fig. 2c

the point on the bottom of the tail base to the point on the tummy side of body. Slip stitch the edges of the tail to the edges of the body through the loops. To give the end of the tail a curl, roll the tip of the tail toward the body and slip stitch the edge of the curl to the tail base. (See Fig. 2c.) Set the body aside.

Step 3. Head

Take two squares and lay them on top of each other, matching edges and points. Stitch a ¼-inch seam starting 1 inch away from one of the points; continue around all edges, ending 1 inch away from the other side of the point you started at. (See Fig. 3.) The points on the opening in the seam will become the neck. Turn head right side out through the seam opening and stuff, so it becomes a pillow about 1–1½ inches deep, with the seam lines being centered on the sides of the head.

The head is placed on the upturned end of the body. On the top side of the body opening, the edges will form a "V" shape. Line up the top of neck "V"-shaped edges to fit into the body's "V." On the bottom side of the head, match the point and edges of the neck opening with the seam lines on the body. Add stuffing as needed to fill in the neck. Pin the points and neck edges so the neck lies smoothly. Slip stitch the edges of the neck to the body around the neck opening

Step 4. Legs

Take 2 squares and lay them on top of each other, matching edges / corners, and stitch a ¼-inch seam on one edge. Open into a rectangle and lay with wrong side up. Fold one of the pipe cleaners in half and lay it on one long edge of the rectangle. Roll the pipe cleaner tightly in the rectangle until you reach the other side of the rectangle. Slip stitch through the loops the long edge to the rolled part of the leg and across each end of the leg. Repeat with 2 more squares. You have two sets of legs.

When you look at the bottom of your chameleon, you will see a diamond shape. This is the tummy. Place one leg on the tummy, with the seam line on the leg centered with head and the back edge of the leg at the seam point closest to the head on the tummy diamond. Slip stitch front and back edges of legs to bottom of body 1 inch out on each side of the leg center seam. (Refer to Clancy's main project photo for leg placement.)

Place the other leg on top of the opposite point of the tummy diamond. Slip stitch the edges of the leg to body like you did for the front legs. Bend the legs down from the ends of the stitching, and to make feet, bend the leg tips out about ½ to ¾ inch from the ends.

Step 5. Face

Using the black fingering weight yarn or embroidery floss, make French knots on the outside points of the head. Use split stitch or outline stitch to embroider the mouth across the front point of the head. If you want to give your chameleon a crest on the top of his head, pinch the fabric on top of the head and stitch through the base of the crest from the front point of the crest to the back point along the length of the crest. You can do the same on the underside of the head to give him a dewlap.

Hide your chameleon on a plant and see how quickly someone discovers him!

Fig. 3

93

PROJECT 18
Ekalaka the Elephant

THE PROJECTS

EKALAKA is named for the county seat of Carter County in far southeastern Montana. The town was named for Ijkalaka, an Oglala Lakota woman who was married to David Harrison Russell, a frontier scout who settled in the area in the late 1800s. Her name translates to "Restless" or "Moving About" in English, which seems very fitting for an elephant!

Although they are made for very different Critters, Ekalaka's legs are made like the legs for Libby the Llama and Eureka the Unicorn.

Supplies Needed
- 144 yards gray DK or light worsted knitting yarn
- 1 yard black fingering weight yarn or embroidery floss for the face
- 1 12-inch pipe cleaner (Optional: this is to stiffen the trunk if you desire.)
- Stuffing

Weave the squares as follows:
18 squares of gray yarn

Step 1. Body

Take 2 squares and lay them on top of each other, matching the corners and edges. Stitch a ¼-inch seam along one edge. Open it into a rectangle. Repeat two more times so you have 3 rectangles of two squares each.

Lay 2 rectangles on top of each other, with right sides together matching edges, corners and seam lines. Stitch a ¼-inch seam along 1 long edge. Open. Now you have a square composed of 4 smaller squares. Take the remaining rectangle and lay it right sides together on one long edge of the square you just made matching the corners, edges, and seam lines. Stitch a ¼-inch seam on 1 long edge. You now have a large rectangle that is 3 squares across and 2 squares high. This is the elephant's back and sides. Lay the rectangle on a flat surface so the right side is up, with 2 squares across by 3 squares high. (See Fig. 1a.)

Take another square and turn it so it's a diamond shape. This will be the elephant's tummy. Match one point on the diamond to the long center seam line down the middle of the rectangle. Pin the point to the seam line. Now match the edges of the tummy square to the edges of the body squares on each side of the seam line, and the corners on the tummy square match the two outside corners on the rectangle. Pin the edges / points and stitch a ¼-inch seam connecting the edges of the body squares to the edges of the tummy square. (See Fig. 1b.)

Take the remaining point on the tummy square and match the point right sides together to the opposite end of the long seamline in the rectangle, so that the right side of the rectangle is enclosed in the folded-over rectangle. Pin the point and match the edges of the tummy square to the edges of the 2 squares on the end of the body rectangle. Pin the edges and stitch a ¼-inch seam, joining the

Fig. 1a

Fig. 1b

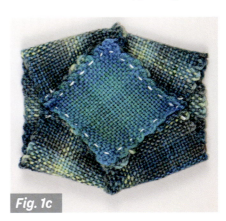

Fig. 1c

95

2 edges of the tummy square to the edges of the 2 squares on the body rectangle. (See Fig. 1c.) You now have a tube that is 2 squares wide and 4 squares around, counting the tummy square. Keep the wrong side out on the body tube.

Adding Ekalaka's bum: Take another square and place it in the opening on one end of the body tube, with the right sides together, lining up one of the points with the seam where the backside and tummy squares come together. Pin. Line up the opposite point of the square to the center of the square (no seam line here) on the opposite side of the tube. Pin / match the rest of the edges / points evenly around the opening, easing as you go. Stitch a ¼-inch seam around the opening, slightly rounding the seam past the points on the bum square.

Adding Ekalaka's chest: Take another square and repeat the steps for the bum on the other open end of the body tube, leaving a small opening between the start and finish of the seam to turn the body and add stuffing.

Turn the body right side out through the opening and stuff the body firmly, so the bum / chest ends and the tummy square bulge outward. Adjust the stuffing so the tummy square is centered on the bottom and the other two seam lines on the body are centered on each side of the elephant's body. Looking at the body from the front, the body on the bum and chest ends should be an oval shape. From the side, the tummy square will

Fig. 2a

bulge out into a potbelly and the back should be flat. Turn under the edges of the seam opening a ¼-inch gap, and slip stitch the edges of the opening closed. Set the body aside.

Step 2. Head

Take 2 squares and place them on top of each other, matching the corners and edges. Start the seam 1½ inches from one corner and stitch a ¼-inch seam around all edges of the squares, stopping 1½ inches away from the corner you started from. (See Fig. 2a.) Turn the head right side out through the opening, and stuff the head until it is shaped like an elongated diamond and is about 1 inch thick. Fold the front and back points of the opening under to the inside of the head until the folded edges meet over the stuffing. Slip stitch the folded edges together. The pointy part of the head is for the trunk, and

Fig. 2b

the opposite wider end, with the folded edges you just stitched, is the top of the head. (See Fig. 2b.)

Take another square, and rolling from one edge, create a cone-shaped tube with a wider opening on one end (upper part of the trunk) and very small opening on the other end (tip of the trunk). (See Fig. 2c.) After rolling

Fig. 2c

the trunk shape, the final position of the looped edge should be on the opposite side of the trunk from the point on the wider opening. Slip stitch the looped edge to the rolled portion of the trunk.

Take the pipe cleaner and cut it in half, so you have 2 6-inch-long pieces. Save one pipe cleaner piece for another project. On the remaining piece of pipe cleaner, turn each cut end under until the pipe cleaner is slightly shorter than the trunk length, from the point on the wide end to the trunk tip. Folding under the ends of the pipe cleaner piece keeps the sharp cut ends of the pipe cleaner from poking through the fabric of the trunk. Twist the folded ends around the pipe cleaner to secure ends. Insert the pipe cleaner into the wide end of the trunk, to the tip of the trunk. Adjust the pipe cleaner length if necessary, so the pipe cleaner is completely covered by the trunk. Tack the pipe cleaner end to the back / seam side of the trunk at the wider opening.

Insert the narrow end of the head into the wider opening on the trunk, with the top point of the trunk centered on the head and the trunk seam toward the underside of the head. Pin the edges. Slip stitch through the loops all the way around the wide end of the trunk, securing the top of the trunk to the head. Set the head aside.

Step 3. Legs
Ekalaka's legs are made like the legs for Libby the Llama and Eureka the Unicorn.

(Refer to "Cone" on page 21 for step-by-step photos for constructing the legs.)

Take a square and fold it into a triangle. Stitch a ¼-inch seam along one edge from fold to point. Turn it right side out and stuff firmly, so the foot end (stitched point) widens out. My elephant legs are about 2½ inches long from the open end point to the bottom of the foot and ¾ inch across at the bottom. Repeat with 3 more squares. You now have 4 legs.

Place the legs with the seam side of the leg toward the body on each side of Ekalaka's body, and the open end point against the body. The leg seam line matches the seam point of the tummy seam. The front edge of the leg opening meets the seam lines around the chest, and for the bum, the back edges of the legs meet the bum / body seam line. Adjust stuffing so the tops of the legs and body are well stuffed and bulge out. Slip stitch through the loops around the top edges of the leg to the body. Make sure all legs are the same height!

Step 4. Placing the Head
Place the backside of the head on the chest, so the top of the head is about 1 to 1½ inches above the height of the back. Slip stitch the edges of the back of the head to the chest where they touch.

Step 5. Adding the Ears
Take one square and stitch a running stitch (knot the end of the yarn) around 1 corner ¼-inch from the looped edge for about 1½ inches total. Pull the running stitch yarn tight to make gathers. Do not cut the stitching yarn. Using the same stitching yarn on the yarn needle, slip stitch the gathered portion of the ear to one side of the upper part of the head. Repeat these steps for the other ear. To make the ears stick out on the sides of the head, tack stitch the ear square's corner that is opposite the gathered end to the shoulder of the elephant.

Step 6. Tail and Face
Tail option 1: For the tail, cut 4 lengths of yarn, each 6 inches long. Make a bundle with all the yarn lengths equal, and tie an overhand knot on one end. Secure the knotted end with a pin pushed into a couch pillow. Divide the yarn into 2 sets of 2 pieces of yarn each. Twist, twist, twist 2 of the yarns together and pin the end to the pillow. Now twist, twist, the other 2 yarns together. Hold both twisted lengths next to each other, tie an overhand knot about 3 inches away from the first knot, and release. The yarns will twist together, making a lovely tail about 2 inches long. Trim one end of the yarn very close to the knot and stitch this knot to the top of the bum at the seam line. Trim the yarn on the other end of the tail about a ¼ inch away from the knot.

Tail option 2: Cut 3 lengths of yarn about 6 inches each. Tie overhand knot on one end of the bundle of yarn. Braid the ends together until you have a tail about 2 inches long. Secure the end of the braid with another overhand knot.

Face: Stitch French knots on each side of the head, using the black fingering weight yarn or embroidery floss.

Curl your elephant's trunk upward for good luck!

PROJECT 19
Hobson the Hippo

HOBSON THE HIPPO is named for the town of Hobson, in central Montana just west of Lewistown. Hobson the town was originally established on the shores of the Judith River where a freight wagon route crossed the river. Perfect, since a hippo spends a majority of its life in water.

With his well-stuffed body, "stumpy" legs, and little tail, Hobson makes a most pleasant Critter companion.

Supplies Needed

88 yards of gray DK or light worsted knitting yarn

2 yards of black fingering weight yarn or embroidery floss for the face

Stuffing

Weave the squares as follows:

11 squares of gray yarn

Step 1. Body

Take 2 squares and lay them on top of each other, matching the corners and edges. On one edge stitch a ¼-inch seam. Open. You now have a rectangle composed of 2 squares. Lay right side up. Take 1 more square and lay it on top of one of the squares of the rectangle, with right sides together, matching the corners / edges. Pin outside end edges together and stitch a ¼-inch seam on outside end edges only. Open. You now have a rectangle composed of 3 squares.

Lay the rectangle right side up. Fold the rectangle in half so the narrow 1-square outside ends of the rectangle are on top of each other, with right sides together, matching outer corners and edges. Stitch a ¼-inch seam along the outside end edges. You now have a tube that is 3 squares around and 1 square wide and open on each end. Leave the tube with wrong side on outside.

Bum and chest: Take another square and place it in the opening on one end of the tube, with right sides together. Line up the corners on one edge of this square to match the seam lines on each side of a square in the tube. This side of the tube is now the hippo's back. Pin the points and edges of the square to the tube edges between pins. Now match the opposite-edge center of the inserted square to the seam line on the opposite side of the tube opening. Pin. This side of the tube is now the hippo's belly. Now match the remaining edges of the square to the tube opening, easing and pinning as you go. Stitch a ¼-inch seam around the opening, rounding the seam slightly past the inserted square's corners on the belly side of the tube. This is the bum end of the body. (See Fig. 1.)

Take another square and repeat the process on the other end of the tube, making sure the two corners of the square matched to the seam lines are on the same tube square as the bum end of the body. Leave a small opening between the start and end of the seam connecting this square to the end of the tube. This is the chest end of the body.

Fig. 1

Turn the body right side out through the seam opening. Stuff the body firmly, so it resembles a bulging rectangle with rounded corners, and the bum and chest ends bulge out substantially. (Refer to the main project photo of Hobson.) Turn the edges of the seam opening under and slip stitch the seam opening closed. Set the body aside.

Step 2. Head

Take 2 squares and place them on top of each other, matching the corners and edges. Stitch a ¼-inch seam around 3 edges, starting and ending the seam ½ inch away from the open edge. Turn the head right side out through the opening, and stuff the head so it looks like a pillow about 1 inch thick. On the top square of your pillow, pinch the corners on each side of the open edge together to make an ear on each side. Stitch across the base of the ears from the end of the seam line on the side of the head to the fold on the ear. The square that has the ears on each side is now the top of the head. (See Fig. 2a.)

Add more stuffing to the head so the stuffing is level to the open edges between the ears, the head is about 1½ inches thick, with the seam line running around the sides/front of the head, and the stuffing is level with the opening between the ears. Fold the top square edge between the ears down over the stuffing and then fold up the edge of the square on the bottom of the head, so the looped edges of the head squares meet. Tuck the open corners of the bottom square to the inside of the head behind the ears on the top square. Slip stitch the edges of the head squares together behind the ears and across the top of the head.

To shape the head, on the bottom side of the head, pinch from the outer edges of the head to the center, making a small pleat in the center back of the head. (See Fig. 2b.) Slip stitch the edges of the pleat together once you are pleased with the shape of the head. (See Fig. 2c.) Set the head aside.

Fig. 2a

Fig. 2b

Fig. 2c

Fig. 3a

Fig. 3b

Step 3. Legs

Take a square and fold one edge toward center about 1 ¼ inch. (See Fig. 3a.) Then fold the opposite edge down so the looped edge matches the folded edge. (See Fig. 3b.) Slip stitch the looped edge to the fold.

Starting at a narrow end, roll tightly to the other end until you have a small cylinder. Slip stitch the looped end to the rolled part of the leg. (See Fig. 3c.) Repeat with three more squares so you have 4 legs.

Fig. 3c

Placement of the legs on the body: Place the round ends of the legs on the belly side (seam line is centered on the belly) of the body, so the leg seams are toward the middle of the body. At the bum end, match the outside edge of the back legs to the seam line between the bum and belly. For the chest end, match the outside edge of the legs to the seam line between chest and body. Slip stitch leg tops to belly all the way around each leg top.

Step 4. Attaching the Head to the Body

Center the back pleated side of the head on the chest, so that the bottom of the head is about ¼ inch higher than the bottom (yes, bottom) of the legs. Slip stitch the back of the head to the chest around all the edges where the head and chest touch. (Refer to the main photo of Hobson for placement of the head on the chest.) The bottom edge of the head should jut away from the body, so don't stitch too far forward on the sides when stitching the head to the chest.

Step 5. Tail

Yes, hippos have tails! Their tails are very small for such a large animal. Cut a 16-inch length of the yarn used for the body squares. Fold it in half and then fold it in half again, so you have 4 lengths of yarn, each 4 inches long. Tie an overhand knot very close to the folded end of the yarn. Pin the overhand knot end of the tail to a couch pillow. Now twist 2 of the yarn lengths together. Pin the end to the pillow so the yarn doesn't untwist. Then twist the other two yarn lengths. Now hold the two twisted lengths together and tie an overhand knot about 1 inch away from the first knot. Release the two lengths of twisted yarn, and they will twist together. Trim the yarn ends close to the knots. Place the tail at the top / center of the bum and stitch the top of the tail into place.

Step 6. Face

Using the black fingering weight yarn or embroidery floss, stitch French knots on each side of the head for the eyes. Use a split stitch or outline stitch to make the mouth, using the seam line around the head as a guide.

Hobson is ready to find a nearby river or lake to take a swim!

PROJECT 20
Geraldine the Giraffe

THE PROJECTS

GERALDINE THE GIRAFFE is named for the small town of Geraldine, almost directly east of Great Falls, Montana. The town was founded in 1916 to house a rail stop for the Milwaukee Railroad and was named for the wife (or perhaps the daughter—there is debate because both women had Geraldine as their middle name) of William Rockefeller.

See the note below for weaving the squares for your giraffe with two colors.

Supplies Needed

136 yards of yellow/brown DK yarn

3 yards of brown DK yarn for the mane

1 yard of black fingering weight yarn or embroidery floss for face

5 12-inch-long pipe cleaners

Stuffing

Weave the squares as follows:

17 squares of yellow/brown DK yarn

Note: My giraffe is made of yellow/brown/rust hand-painted yarns. If you don't have a variegated / painted yarn, you can weave your squares with 2 colors instead. Use yellow or gold yarn for the three rounds on the loom (102 total yards needed) and then tie on a brown yarn (34 total yards needed) to weave the square. This will give you a square that is predominantly yellow with spots of brown, kind of like a giraffe's coat. Or reverse the colors so the first 3 rounds are brown and then weave with yellow. Check out Olney the Owl's photo (page 64) to see this type of square.

See the appendix for how to tie on a new color of yarn.

Step 1. Body

Take 2 squares and lay them on top of each other, matching the corners and edges. Stitch a ¼-inch seam along one edge. Open and lay it so the right side is up. You have a rectangle of 2 squares.

Take another square and lay it over one of the squares in the rectangle, matching the corners and edges. Stitch a ¼-inch seam along the outside end edge. Open. You now have a rectangle composed of 3 squares.

Repeat these steps with 3 more squares. You now have 2 rectangles composed of 3 squares each.

Lay the rectangles on top of each other, with the right sides together, matching the seams, outer corners, and edges. Stitch a ¼-inch seam along one long edge. Open. You now have a large rectangle that is 3 squares long and 2 squares high.

Fold the large rectangle in half, so the ends composed of 2 squares are on top of each other, with right sides together, matching the edges, corners, and center seam line. Stitch a ¼-inch seam on the outside end edge composed of 2 squares. You now have a tube that is open on each end and that is 3 squares around and 2 squares high. Leave the tube wrong side out.

Chest: Take another square and place it inside one of the openings in the tube, with right sides together, matching one of the square's points with a seam line in the tube. Pin. Line up the opposite point of the square with the center of the square on the opposite side of the tube opening. Pin. Place the remaining points of the square so the points are centered between the first points. Pin the points. Pin edges of the square to the edges of the tube between pinned points. Stitch a ¼-inch seam around the opening / chest square, easing any fullness as you stitch and rounding the seam past the points of the chest square.

103

Bum: Take another square and place in the remaining opening of the tube, with right sides together. Repeat the pinning / stitching process you did for the chest, ending the seam about 1½ inches before you reach the beginning of the seam to leave a small opening in the seam for stuffing.

Turn the body right side out through the opening in the seam. Stuff the body firmly into an oblong boxlike shape with rounded corners viewed from the side and the bum / chest ends round out and are oval shapes when viewed from the ends of the body. (See Fig. 1.) Turn under the edges of the seam opening and slip stitch the seam opening closed. Set the body aside.

Step 2. Neck

There are 2 parts to the neck—the upper neck and the lower neck.

Upper neck: Take one square and fold in half, matching long edges and corners. On the long edge, whip stitch the edges together through the loops. Do *not* turn inside out. Stuff very firmly.

Lower neck: Take 2 squares and lay them on top of each other, matching the corners and edges. Stitch a ¼-inch seam on one edge, starting at the corner and ending the seam 1 inch away from the next corner. Now, stitch another ¼-inch seam, starting on the point opposite where you started the seam to the first point. Stitch a ¼-inch seam from the corner up to 1 inch

Fig. 1

Fig. 2a

away from same point you ended the first seam at. (See Fig. 2a.) Turn right side out. The smaller opening is opposite a large opening of 2 unstitched edges.

Now take the stuffed upper neck and insert one end into the smaller opening in the lower neck. I find that inserting the upper neck

Fig. 2b

into the wide opening of the lower neck and then continuing through the small opening is easiest. Line up one of the points on the lower neck with the seam line on the upper neck. Line up the seam lines on each side of the lower neck, so the ends of the seam lines are even with the bottom edges of the upper neck. The upper neck will extend about 2½ inches above the points on the lower neck. Pin and slip stitch the lower neck edge through the loops to the upper neck. Firmly stuff the top of the lower neck.

Place the wide opening of the lower neck on one end of the body, centering one of the points of the lower neck on the back, so the point meets the seam line between the body and bum. Pin the point. Place the opposite point of the lower neck on the chest, so the point is about ¾ inch above the lower seam line between the body / chest. Pin the points and lower neck edges to the body, so they lie smoothly on the body. Place additional stuffing under the portion of the lower neck that is on the giraffe's back, to create a shoulder slope / hump. Slip stitch through the lower neck loops to the back of the giraffe first. If necessary, repin the front point on the chest and adjust the stuffing between the chest and the lower neck point. Continue stitching the edge of the neck around the chest point of the lower neck. The stuffing needs to be firm so the neck stands erect. Add more stuffing through the top opening of the upper neck, if necessary, until the neck is firm enough to stand erect. (See Fig. 2b.) Set the body aside.

Step 3. Head

Take another square and fold into a triangle. Stitch a ¼-inch seam, starting 1 inch away from the folded edge, along one edge, around the point, and down the other edge, ending 1 inch away from the fold. (See Fig. 3a.) Turn right side out through one of the openings. The flaps on each side are the ears. Stuff the stitched point firmly to shape the head.

Fig. 3a

With the head facing you, insert your thumb in one ear opening and your pointer finger in the other opening. Pinch ears together so they meet over the top of the head. Stitch across the bottom edges of the ears through all layers. (See Fig. 3b.) The ears will stick straight back at this point.

Place the head on top of the neck, so the stuffed point (nose) is toward the front of the giraffe and the ears are pointed toward the back of your giraffe. Slip stitch the bottom of the head to the top of the neck.

Now separate the ears by placing a finger between them to make the insides of the ears face forward and stick out on each side of the head. Slip stitch the fronts of the base of the ears to the back of the head to hold the ears in place. (See the main project photo for reference.)

Fig. 3b

Step 4. Legs

Upper legs: Each leg consists of two squares. Take one square and fold it into a triangle. Stitch a ¼-inch seam on one edge, starting at the point and stitching to 1 inch away from the fold. (See Fig. 4a.) Turn right side out. Repeat with 3 more squares. You now have 4 cone-shaped upper legs open at both ends of the cone.

Fig. 4a

Lower legs: Fold a 12-inch pipe cleaner in half. Take another square and roll it tightly around the folded end of the pipe cleaner. Slip stitch the looped edge of the square to the rolled portion of the lower leg. Slip stitch the bottom loops together for the foot, making sure to enclose the folded end of the pipe cleaner in the rolled square. (See Fig. 4b.)

Joining leg sections: Insert the covered pipe cleaner end of the lower leg into the wider opening of the upper leg and continue pushing the lower leg through the upper leg and exiting through the smaller opening of the upper leg. Rotate the lower leg so the seam line of the upper leg matches the seam line of the lower leg and the top end of the upper leg overlaps the top of the lower leg by ¼ inch at the seam lines side of the legs. The point on

Fig. 4b

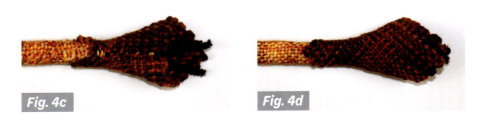
Fig. 4c Fig. 4d

the small opening of the upper leg will be centered on the front of the lower leg. Pin the edges and slip stitch through the loops the bottom of the upper leg to the top of the lower leg. (See Figs. 4c and 4d.) Repeat for three more legs.

Fold the pipe cleaner ends in the large opening of the upper legs 90 degrees toward the seam side of the leg, so the bend is about even with the edge of the seamed side of the leg. Stuff all upper legs firmly to the top point of the open end and around the pipe cleaner.

Refer to main project photo for leg placement on the body.

Back legs: Place a leg on the body so the top point is centered on the seam line between the body squares and the bum squares. Stick the bent ends of the pipe cleaner into the body. Pin the edges of the upper leg to the body. Place another leg on the opposite side of the body, checking to make sure the legs are even. The legs should measure about 3 inches from the bottom of the body to the bottom of the leg. Now place the front legs.

Front legs: Center the top point of the front legs on the seam line between the body and chest, making sure the front legs are the same length as the back legs, and poke the pipe cleaner ends into the body. Pin the edges of the upper leg to the body. Repeat with other front leg.

Once you have all the legs placed on the body, confirm that all the legs are even with each other, adjust stuffing in the upper legs as necessary, and then slip stitch through the loops the openings of the upper legs to the body.

Step 4. Tail, Mane, Horns, and Face

Tail: Cut 2 7-inch-long lengths of the brown/yellow yarn. Lay the two lengths next to each other and fold in half. Tie an overhand knot on the end with the fold, so you have 4 lengths of yarn. Take 2 of the yarn lengths and twist them together. Pin the end to a couch pillow to keep it from untwisting. Now twist the other 2 lengths of yarn. Now hold the 2 twisted lengths of yarn

together, tie an overhand knot on the cut ends, release, and let the lengths twist together. Trim the cut ends about ½ inch from the knot. Place the tail centered on the back at the seam line between the bum and body. Stitch the top of the tail to the body.

Mane: The mane is created with the brown yarn. Thread a yarn needle and stitch a series of small loops about ¼ inch high, starting at the base of the head and centered down the neck, ending just above the shoulders of your giraffe.

Horns: Cut the remaining pipe cleaner in half so you have two 6-inch pieces. Save one piece of the pipe cleaner for another project. Poke one end of the pipe cleaner through the top of the head, slightly forward and between the ears, for about ½ inch between where the pipe cleaner enters and exits the head. Fold the ends of the pipe cleaner up 90 degrees. Now fold the cut ends over, so the horns measure ½ inch long from fold to the top of the head. Trim cut ends of the pipe cleaner, if necessary, so the cut ends are against the top of the head and each horn is a doubled length of pipe cleaner measuring about ½ inch long. Starting from the base of the horns, insert the yarn needle between the pipe cleaner folds on a horn from the backside, bring the yarn around one side of a horn, and insert the needle in the center again. Now bring the yarn around the opposite side of the horn and insert the needle in the center again to make a figure 8. Keep repeating the figure 8 between sides of the horn until the horn is completely covered. Insert the needle down through the middle of the figure 8 crosses between the 2 sides of the horn, pull the yarn through, and cut the yarn very close to the horn. Repeat for other horn.

Face: Using black fingering weight yarn or embroidery floss, make French knots on each side of the head for the eyes. If you want to add eyelashes, knot the end of the yarn you used for the eyes so there is about a ½-inch tail. Poke your needle into the head just behind one of the eyes, push the needle through the head, and exit the needle just behind the eye on the opposite side, pulling the yarn so the knot is snugged up to the fabric behind the first eye. Now tie a knot in the yarn where the needle exited, and tighten the knot so it is snug against the head behind the second eye. Cut yarn on needle, leaving a ½-inch tail. Unravel the 2 tails to make eyelashes. Trim the eyelashes to ¼ inch or your desired length.

Introduce Geraldine to Ekalaka (page 94), Hobson (page 98), and Clancy (page 90) to complete your African herd!

PROJECT 21
Rosebud the Rabbit

THE PROJECTS

AS I SCANNED A MAP of Montana, searching for a name for this kit, I found the town of Rosebud, located on the Rosebud River in Rosebud County. Since my rabbit is also made of rosy colored yarn, it really felt like someone was trying to tell me something—so I listened.

Supplies Needed

- 128 yards DK or light worsted knitting yarn for the body
- 16 yards pink DK or light worsted yarn for the inside of the ears
- Stuffing
- Black fingering weight yarn or embroidery floss for the face
- 1-inch-wide ruler or piece of cardboard for making the tail pom-pom

Weave the squares as follows:

- 16 squares of the body yarn color of your choice
- 2 squares of the pink yarn for inside of ears

Step 1. Body

Take 2 body squares and lay them on top of each other, matching the corners and edges. Stitch a ¼-inch seam on one edge. Open and lay so the right side is up. Place another square over one of the squares in the rectangle, matching the corners and edges. Stitch a ¼-inch seam on the outside end edge, so that you have a rectangle composed of 3 squares. Set aside.

Take 2 more body squares and lay them on top of each other, matching the corners and edges. Stitch a ¼-inch seam on one edge. Open. You have a rectangle composed of 2 squares.

Lay the rectangle composed of 3 squares on a flat surface, with the right side up. Now lay the rectangle composed of 2 squares on top of the middle and right-hand squares of the larger rectangle, with right sides together, matching the edges, seams, and outside corner. Stitch a ¼-inch seam on one long edge of the rectangles. Open. You now have a 2-square rectangle above the 3-square rectangle connected on one edge. Lay right side up on flat surface.

Lay another single body square with right sides together on the middle square of the 3-square rectangle, matching edges. Stitch a ¼-inch seam along edge of this single square and the middle square in the large rectangle. Open. The configuration of the rectangles should be a 2-square rectangle above the 3-square rectangle and a single square at the bottom center of the 3-square rectangle. (See Fig. 1a.) Take note of the open square

Fig. 1a

109

shapes in the upper left corner and the lower right corner.

Lay the fabric on a flat surface, with the right side up in the same configuration as Fig. 1a, with the 2-square rectangle at the top, 3-square rectangle in the middle, and the single square at the bottom.

Now, take the outside edge of the square farthest on the right on the middle 3-square rectangle and fold it over so the bottom edge of this square matches the outside / right-hand side edge of the single square at the bottom and the right sides of the squares are together.

Fig. 1b

Stitch a ¼-inch seam joining these two edges.

In the upper left-hand corner of the photo, there's another empty square shape. Fold the left-hand edge of the 2-square rectangle over so it matches the top edge of the farthest left square of the 3-square rectangle, with the right sides of the

Fig. 1d

Fig. 1c

squares together. Stitch a ¼-inch seam joining the two edges. (See Fig. 1b.) Turn the body right side out.

Stuff the body firmly, shaping it so the back is arched a bit. The side of the body with the opening is the belly. Stuff the body so the belly is flatter than the back and the opening in the body is centered on the belly. All the seam lines will now be on the diagonal when you look at the body from the sides, top, and belly. The arched side is the back of the rabbit and the center square on the back will be a diamond shape when you look down on the back.

Once you stuff the body, you will notice that the opening has a point that fits into the indent on the opposite side of the opening. Place the point of the square over the stuffing so it fits into the inverse point on the other side of the opening. Fold under the edges around the opening and slip stitch the edges of the opening together. The body will look like a football shape that is a little flat on the belly side. (See Fig. 1c.)

Select one end of the body for the rabbit's bum. Press the pointy end of the football on this end

toward the inside of the body, so the bum will be nicely rounded. Slip stitch the folded edges together on each side of the dent created where you pushed the fabric to the inside. (See Fig. 1d.) Don't worry that the folded-edges seam doesn't look perfect, because the tail will cover this area. Set the body aside.

Step 2. Head

Take 2 more body squares and lay them on top of each other, matching the corners and edges. Stitch a ¼-inch seam starting 1 inch away from a corner, down the edge, then slightly rounding the seam past the next corner. Continue the seam to the next corner, stitching to a point,

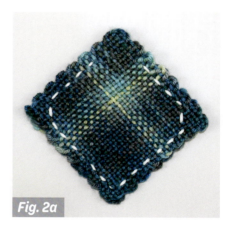
Fig. 2a

Fig. 2b

THE PROJECTS

Fig. 2c

Fig. 3a

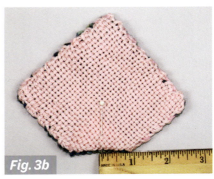
Fig. 3b

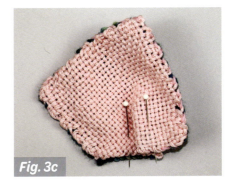
Fig. 3c

Fig. 3d

then continue to the next corner, slightly rounding the seam past this corner, then ending the seam 1 inch away from the corner where you started the seam. (See Fig. 2a.)

Turn the head right side out through the seam opening and stuff firmly. (See Fig. 2b.) Fold one point of the seam opening over the stuffing and then fold the opposite point over the first point, so the points overlap over the stuffing. Slip stitch through the loops of the top point to the fabric of the bottom point to close the opening. The head will be a pear shape, with the narrow end forming the nose and the wider end the top of the head. (See Fig. 2c.) Place the head on the upper slope of the chest (pointy) end of the body with the wide part of the head toward the rabbit's back and the nose end toward the front of the body. Slip stitch the backside of the head to the front of the body along all edges that touch.

Step 3. Ears

Take one body square and one of the pink squares. Fold down one point on each square 1 inch, measured from point to fold. (See Fig. 3a.) Lay the squares on top of each other so the folded points are on the inside and on top of each other. Slip stitch the folded edges together and then whip stitch through the loops around the remaining edges. Repeat for the second ear.

Lay an ear flat on your work surface, with the pink side facing you and the flat folded edges nearest you. Mark the center of the folded-over edges. (See Fig. 3b.) Hold the ear with the pink side facing you, and fold the ear so that the points on each side meet at the center of the ear at the pin and the folded-over edges at the bottom are even with each other. You will have a pleat of fabric on the backside of the ear. (See Fig. 3c.) Flatten the pleated fabric on the back of the ear, so the bottom edges of the pleat on the backside of the ear are even with the front edges of the pink side of the ear. Pin the edges. You should have a flattened pleat on the backside of the ear and the concave side of the pleat on the pink side. Slip stitch the bottom edges of the pleat to the front edges of the ear, so the bottom of the ear is straight across. (See Fig. 3d.)

Position the ears on each side on the back of the head, so the tips

111

of the ears point to the rear of the body and the pink side faces out. Slip stitch bottom flat edges of the ear to the head. (Refer to the main project photo for placement.) Set the body aside.

Step 4. Legs

(Refer to "Basic Legs" on page 19 for step-by-step photos for constructing the legs.)

Front legs: Take a body square and fold in half. Stitch a ¼-inch seam down the long edge and then one short edge. Turn right side out. Push the edges of the open end to the inside of the leg until the leg measures 2½ inches long. Stuff the leg through the opening. Slip stitch the opening closed from seam line out. Repeat for second front leg. Place the legs on the lower edge of the front of the body, so the front ends of the legs are even with the front point on the chest and the long seam line is down. Slip stitch edges of leg to the body where they touch. (Refer to the main project photo for placement of front legs.)

Back legs: Take another body square and fold it in half. Stitch a ¼-inch seam along the long edge and across one short end. Turn right side out and stuff. Match the edges of the opening and whip stitch through the loops, starting from the seam line on one edge and across the opening to close the end of the leg. Repeat with a second square. These are the lower parts of the back legs. Position the legs on each side of the body on the belly side, with long seam lines down and with the back ends of the legs lining up with the bum end of the body. The bottom-seam-side edge of the legs should be about ½ inch lower than the bottom edge of the body. Slip stitch the top edges of the leg to the bottom of the body. Refer to the main project photo for placement of the back legs.

Upper back leg: Take another body square and position it on the rear of the body, so one point of the square lines up with the seam line point on the side of the body. Turn the edges of the square on each side of the point under about ¼ inch and pin the edges to the body, using the body seam line as a guide for upper leg placement, tucking the points under when you reach them. Fold the lowest point of the upper leg square back to the inside of the upper leg to match the edge of the lower back leg, so the upper leg / lower leg edges meet. The square will not lie flat against the body. Slip stitch the edges of the upper leg to the body, starting by the lower leg and working your way around until you reach the back end of the lower leg. The folded-under point of the upper leg is still open. Stuff the upper leg through the opening so it bulges out from the body. Once you are happy with the shape, slip stitch the folded under edge of the upper leg to the top edge of the lower leg.

Step 5: Face and Tail:

Tail: With the body yarn, make a pom-pom by winding the yarn 12 times (or more, if you desire a fluffier tail) around a 1-inch-wide ruler or piece of cardboard. Thread a piece of scrap body yarn onto a yarn needle. Slide the yarn needle under the wraps on the ruler and pull the yarn to the ruler edge opposite the cut end of the yarn. Tie the scrap yarn tightly around the yarn loops with a knot. Trim the tied ends next to the knot. Cut the other end of the pom-pom. To make a nice, fluffy tail, unply the lengths of yarn in the pom-pom by slightly untwisting a length of yarn, insert the tip of the yarn needle between the plies, and pull the needle tip to the cut end. Position the tail on the bum, covering where you made that pleat earlier to round out the bum, and stitch the tail to the body through the pom-pom tie yarn.

Face: Using black fingering weight yarn or embroidery floss, stitch the eyes and mouth, using an outline stitch or split stitch. Use a satin stitch outlined with a split stitch to make the nose.

Rosebud is ready to hop through the grass (or into someone's arms)!

THE PROJECTS

PROJECT 22
Cascade the Cat

THE PROJECTS

WHEN I CAME UP WITH THE IDEA of a Cat Critter, I had already decided it would be named for Cascade County. "Cascade" means waterfall in French, and the county was named for the waterfalls on the Missouri River. Now, it may seem odd to name a cat for a water feature since cats aren't known to be fond of water. Truthfully, I just really liked the sound of Cascade with Cat.

Cascade includes typical feline features like whiskers and a long, curving tail.

Supplies Needed
136 yards of gray DK knitting yarn
Black felt for the eyes / nose (template for eyes / nose is in the appendix)
Stuffing
Black sewing thread and needle
Black fingering weight yarn or embroidery floss for the face

Weave the squares as follows:
17 squares of gray yarn

Step 1. Body

Take two squares and lay them on top of each other, matching the edges and corners. Stitch a ¼-inch seam on one edge. Open. You have a rectangle 2 squares long. Lay this rectangle on a flat surface, with the right side up, and place another square on top of the right-hand square, matching the edges and corners. Stitch a ¼-inch seam on the outside end edge to make a rectangle 3 squares long and 1 square high. This rectangle becomes the tummy / back portion of the body. Set aside.

Take another two squares and lay them on top of each other, matching edges / corners. Stitch a ¼-inch seam on one edge. Open. You have a rectangle 2 squares long by 1 square high. This rectangle will be Cascade's neck.

Lay the longer 3-square body rectangle on a flat surface, with the right side up. Lay the shorter 2-square neck rectangle on top, so the right sides of the rectangles are together and the neck rectangle's seam line matches the center of the middle square of the longer body rectangle. Stitch a ¼-inch seam along one long edge, joining the rectangles. Open and lay flat, with the right side up. (See Fig. 1a.)

Now fold the joined rectangles in half at the center seam on the

Fig. 1a

Fig. 1b

115

Fig. 1c

the center of the body square on the other side of the tube opening. Pin the remaining points (all should stick up about ½ inch over the body edge) and match the edges of the square to the edges of the tube opening between the pinned points. Stitch a ¼-inch seam around the opening, easing as you go and rounding the seam past the points. This end of the body is the cat's bum. Turn the body right side out through the neck opening. Stuff the body firmly through the neck opening, rounding out the curved side of the body for the back / bum. (See Fig. 1c.) Set the body aside.

edges. Starting at a point, stitch a ¼-inch seam down one edge, around the next point, and down the next edge to the next point. Leave the remaining two edges unstitched. (See Fig. 2b.) This is the face.

Fig. 2b

Fig. 2c

neck rectangle, with the right sides together so the outside edges / corners of the neck squares meet and the outside edges / corners of the body squares meet. Pin. Start a ¼-inch seam at the top edge of the neck and continue the seam to the seam between the neck and body rectangles. Angle the seam across the upper corner of the body squares to about the halfway point of the square, then continue stitching a ¼-inch seam to the end. (Refer to Fig. 1b for the seam stitching line.) You now have a pear-ish-shaped tube open on both ends. Leave the body tube wrong side out.

Take another square and place it inside the larger end of the body tube, with the right sides together. Pin one corner of the square to the back seam line of the body tube, so the square's point sticks up about ½ inch above the body edge. Pin the opposite point of the square to

Step 2. Head

Take another square and pinch one corner, matching the edges on each side of the corner. Make a tacking stitch about ½ inch down from the point through both layers of fabric to make a small pleat. This is one ear. Repeat on the point across from the first ear. (See Fig. 2a.) This square is the backside of the head, and the side of the ear with the pleat is the right side of the square. Set aside.

Lay 2 squares on top of each other, matching the corners and

Fig. 2a

Lay the face on top of the ear / back-of-head square with right sides together, with the seam lines on the face centered on each side of back-of-head square below the ears. Pin. Center the top point of the face to the back of head between the ears. Pin. Center the bottom point of the face on the bottom edge of the back-of-head square. Pin. Center the lower points on the back-of-head square between the pinned points on the

116

THE PROJECTS

face. Center and pin the bases of the back-of-head ear points to the face on each side of the upper face. Match the remaining edges between the pinned points from ear to ear around the face / back-of-head squares. Stitch a ¼-inch seam starting from outside edge of one ear, around the face / head, and ending at the outside edge of the opposite ear, leaving an opening between the ears for stuffing. Turn the head right side out and stuff firmly. (See Fig. 2c.)

After stuffing the head, fold the top open point back between the ears to the inside of the head until the fold edge meets edge of the back-of-head square between the ears. Slip stitch the folded edge to the back of the head between the ears.

Place the head on top of the neck opening, so the center back of the head matches the back seam line of the curved side of the body. Slip stitch the neck edge to the bottom of the head around the neck opening. Set the body aside.

Step 3. Legs

(Refer to "Basic Leg" on page 19 for step-by-step photos for constructing the back legs and lower front legs.)

Take a square and fold in half. Stitch a ¼-inch seam along the long edge and across one short edge. Turn right side out through the opening and stuff, shaping the leg so it is flatter rather than round, with the long seam on one edge. Match the edges of the opening so

the seam line is on one edge of the leg. Slip stitch the opening closed. Repeat with another square for the other back leg. Set back legs aside.

Front legs—lower leg: The front legs use two squares each—one square for the upper leg and one square for the lower leg. For the lower legs, fold a square in half and stitch a ¼-inch seam along the long edge and across one short

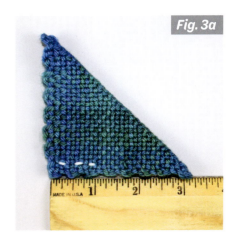
Fig. 3a

Fig. 3b

edge just like you did for the back legs. Turn right side out and stuff into a rounded shape. Repeat with another square for the other lower leg.

Front legs—upper leg: Take another square and fold it into a triangle. Starting at the top point of the triangle, stitch a ¼-inch seam for 1 inch along one edge of the triangle. (See Fig. 3a.) Turn right side out. Insert one of the lower legs into the larger opening and then through the smaller opening made with the 1-inch seam, matching the seam on the upper leg to the long seam on the lower leg. The joined leg should be about 5 inches long, and the lower point on the upper leg should be about 1½ inches from

the bottom edge of the lower leg. (See Fig. 3b.) Pin and slip stitch the bottom edge of the upper leg to the top of the lower leg all the way around the leg. Stuff the upper leg firmly. Fold the top point of the upper leg over, stuffing toward the back of the leg, matching the edges of the point to the bottom edges of the large opening. Slip stitch the looped edges of the folded-over point to the looped edges of the upper leg. Fold the bottom end of the lower leg up about 1 inch to form a foot. Slip stitch the edges of the fold together to make an "ankle." Repeat for second front leg.

Refer to the main project photo for leg and tail placement and face details.

117

Place the back legs on the bottom of the body so the legs lie flat, with the back narrow edge at about the halfway point of the bottom of the body and the leg seams on the body-side edge of the leg. Slip stitch the back-leg edges to the body where they touch.

Place the top of the front legs at an angle, so the front corner of the leg matches the seam line between the neck / body and the back top corner of the leg is about ½ inch above the neck / body seam line. Slip stitch top of the leg to body where they touch.

Step 4. Tail

Lay the last two squares on top of each other, matching the corners and edges. Stitch a ¼-inch seam along one edge. Open into a rectangle. Place the rectangle wrong side up on a flat surface. Starting on one long edge, roll the rectangle to the opposite edge, so you wind up with a roll that is about ¾ inch across. Slip stitch the edge loops to the side of the roll and across both ends of the tail. Slip stitch one end of the tail to the lower bum. Curl the other end of the tail up and stitch to the side of the body, if desired.

Step 5. Face

Eyes and nose: Using the face patterns in the appendix, cut 2 eyes and a nose out of black felt. Place the eyes on each side of the upper face just below the ears. Slip stitch around the edges, using black sewing thread. Center the nose on the stuffed point of the face and slip stitch around the edges with sewing thread.

Mouth: Using the black fingering weight yarn or embroidery floss, use an outline or split stitch to embroider Cascade's mouth.

Whiskers: Thread your yarn needle with leftover yarn from the body squares and tie a knot about 2 inches from the cut end. Poke the needle tip through the nose from one side of the nose to the opposite side. Tie another knot so the knot is next to the nose on the other side. Cut the yarn, leaving a 2-inch-long tail. That's one pair of whiskers. Repeat two more times.

Done! A nice added touch could be to add a collar with a bell around Cascade's neck, so the other Critters know she is on the prowl!

THE PROJECTS

PROJECT 23
Ovando the Octopus

AS I DESIGNED CRITTERS, I really wanted to make an aquatic critter, and in my opinion, the coolest critter in the sea is the octopus. Octopuses are masters of disguise, can slip through the smallest spaces, and are really smart to boot! I looked for a Montana river or lake that starts with an "O" (for octopus), but no luck. However, the Blackfoot River runs through the census-designated area of Ovando, which sounds good with Octopus, so that worked for me!

To make Ovando more special, you can adjust the shape and tips of his legs.

Supplies Needed

72 yards dark gray DK or light worsted knitting yarn

24 yards aqua DK or light worsted knitting yarn

Aqua felt for eyes

Stuffing

Blue sewing thread and a needle to sew eyes to body

Weave the squares as follows:

Weave 12 squares, using the gray yarn for the 3 rounds of yarn wound on the loom, then tie on the aqua yarn and weave with the aqua. See the appendix for instructions on changing yarn color in the squares for weaving.

Step 1. Legs

Refer to "Cone" on page 21 for step-by-step photos for constructing the leg shape.

Take a square and fold it into a triangle. Stitch a ¼-inch seam on one edge from point to fold. Turn the right side out and center the seam below the open point. You have a cone shape. Repeat with 7 more squares for a total of 8 legs.

Stuff all the legs. (See Fig. 1a.) Lay two legs next to each other, with the seam side facing up. Tack stitch the top edges of the legs together about ½ inch up from the flat lower edge of the opening. Continue tacking the legs together until all 8 are stitched together.

Now place the two end legs together and tack stitch the outside edges of these legs together. You now have a circle of legs. (See Fig. 1b.) Set the legs aside.

Fig. 1a

Fig. 1b

121

Step 2. Body / Head

Take two squares and lay them on top of each other, matching the corners and edges. Stitch a ¼-inch seam along two adjoining edges. Open onto large cone-like shape. Leave the wrong sides out.

Take a third square and lay it inside the opening of the cone shape, with right sides together, matching a point of the square to a seam line on the larger cone shape. Pin. Match the edges of the square on each side of the point. Stitch a ¼-inch seam on each side of the pinned point.

Now match the remaining square point and edges to the opposite seam line / edges of the large cone shape. Stitch a ¼-inch seam around the edges, leaving a small opening at the end of the seam for stuffing. Turn right side out through the opening. Stuff the body firmly, shaping it into a pear shape, with the narrow end to be attached to the legs and the wide end to be the top of the body/head. Fold under the edges of the seam opening and slip stitch seam opening closed. (See Fig. 2.)

If the top corners of the body / head are too pointy for your tastes, poke those points to the inside of the body and slip stitch the new folded edges together to give the top of the body a rounder shape.

Step 3. Attaching the Body to the Legs

Place the circle of legs on a flat surface, with the seam side of the legs facing down. Look at the body; you will see "Y"-shaped seams on opposite sides of the body—these "Y"-shaped seams are at the front and back of body. Place the pointed end of the body into the opening in the circle of legs. Place the wrong sides of the points of the leg openings against the lower sides of the body, so the points on the legs overlap the bottom of the body by about ½ inch, pinning and adjusting the position of the body as you go. When you are happy with how the body sits on the legs, slip stitch through the loops around all the leg edges to the body. If there are any gaps between the tops of the legs, slip stitch those closed as well.

Step 4. Underside of the Body / Legs

Turn the octopus over and firmly stuff the opening on the underside of the body. Take the remaining square and place it over the opening / stuffed area. Match the points on the square with seams on 4 legs that are an equal distance apart from each other, so there is one leg between each of the legs that matches the points on the square.

Fig. 4a

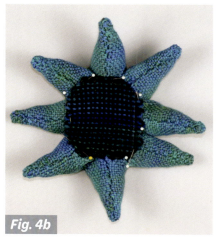
Fig. 4b

(See Fig. 4a.) Fold the points on the square under to the stuffing side, so the fold line of the folded back square point matches the edges of the legs. Pin the folded edge to the leg. Do this for all 4 points of the square. Between the pinned corners, match and pin the edges of the square to the edges of the legs. Pin. The square is now an octagon. Slip stitch the looped edges of the legs to the edges of the body bottom, making sure all edges are closed, and if necessary, slip stitch between the legs to completely close the legs and bottom of the body. (See Fig. 4b.)

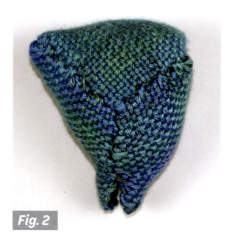
Fig. 2

Step 5. Face

Using bright aqua felt, cut out 2 eyes, using the pattern template in the appendix. Place the eyes on the front of the body, with the bottom of the eyes about ½ inch above the legs. Stitch the eyes to the body, using sewing thread.

    Optional: To give your octopus a little more personality, you can fold the tips of some of the legs to the side or up and slip stitch the edges of the folds together to hold the leg bend in place.

Ovando is ready to explore the world with you.

PROJECT 24
Pablo the Peacock

PABLO THE PEACOCK brings to mind the bright colors Pablo Picasso used in his paintings. And there's a town named Pablo in northwestern Montana. It's home to the Salish Kootenai College, named for two Native American tribes, and is the seat of government for the Flathead Indian Reservation. The town was established in 1917 and named for Michel Pablo, a man known for his efforts to save the American bison (a.k.a. buffalo) from extinction.

Unlike most of the Critters, Pablo uses a twill weave!

Supplies Needed

76 yards of blue-green DK or light worsted knitting yarn for body

50 yards bright multicolored yarn for tail and wings

2 yards black and 2 yards white fingering weight yarn or embroidery floss for face details

Stuffing

Weave the squares as follows:

Weave 8 squares of blue-green yarn for body

Weave 5 squares of bright multicolored yarn for tail feathers

Weave 2 squares of blue-green body yarn and multicolored yarn for the wings in twill weave. (See the appendix for instructions on how to weave twill on a pin loom.)

Step 1. Body

Refer to "Small Closed Tube" on page 20 for step-by-step photos for constructing the body.

Take 2 blue-green squares and lay them on top of each other, matching the corners and edges. Stitch a ¼-inch seam on one edge. On the opposite edge, stitch a ¼-inch seam. You will now have a tube open on each end. Leave the tube with the wrong side out.Take a third body square and place it over one of the open ends, with the right sides together, matching one point to one of the tube seams so that the point is about ½ inch above the edge of the tube. Pin. On the opposite side of the square, match the point to the other seam on the tube, again so the point is about ½ inch above the edge of the tube. Match the 2 remaining points to the centers of the squares on each side of the tube and, again, ½ inch of the point above the edge of the tube. Pin the points. Match / pin edges of

the tube and square between the pinned points around the opening. Stitch a ¼-inch seam around the opening, easing in any excess fabric on the square. If you have some gathers in this seam, it doesn't matter! This end is the peacock's bum, and you will be covering it with feathers.

Turn the body through the tube opening so the right side is out. Stuff the body firmly, so the bum bulges out a bit. On the open end of the tube, stitch a running stitch around the opening ¼ inch from the opening edges, leaving a 2-inch tail at the beginning. Pull on both ends of the stitching yarn like a drawstring to close the opening. Tie the stitching yarn with a knot and trim yarn ends close to the knot. This end of the body is Pablo's chest. Set the body aside.

SWATCH CRITTERS FROM THE PIN LOOM

Fig. 2

Step 2. Head and Neck

Head: Take one blue-green square and fold it into a triangle. Now fold it in half again, matching looped edges into a smaller triangle, and fold in half again into an even smaller triangle, so the folded edges are stacked up together and the looped edges are stacked up together on the sides of the small triangle. Slip stitch the looped edges together and then slip stitch the folded edges together. Set aside.

(Refer to "Neck Shape" on page 21 for step-by-step photos for constructing the neck.)

Neck: Take a blue-green square and fold one point down ½ inch. Now fold into a triangle with the folded point on the outside, matching edges and points. Stitch a ¼-inch seam along one edge from folded-back point's edge to the point at the top of the triangle. Turn the neck right side out so the folded-back point and seam edges are now on the inside. The small opening is the top of the neck. Stuff the neck firmly from the small opening all the way to the edges of the wider opening that is the chest end of the neck. Lay the body on a flat surface, with the seam lines on each side of the body. Place the large neck opening on the chest (gathered end) of the body so the neck seam line matches the center back of the body. Place the point of the neck opening so it is centered between the seam lines on the underside of the body and is about even with the bottom of the body / chest. Pin the edges of the neck to the front of the body so the edges lay smoothly and the gathers on the front of the body are completely covered by the base of the neck. Slip stitch through the loops the edges of the neck to the front of the body.

Take the head and place it on the top of the neck so that one stitched edge matches the top of the neck and the other stitched edge matches the back of the neck. Slip stitch the bottom edges of the head to the top edges of the neck. (See Fig. 2.) Set the body aside.

Step 3. Tail

The tail uses 3 squares in blue-green yarn and 5 squares of the Bright multi-colored yarn.

(Refer to "Cone" on page 21 for step-by-step photos for constructing the feathers.)

Feathers: Take a blue-green square and fold it into a triangle. Whip stitch through the loops one edge of the triangle from the fold to the point. Flatten it into a cone shape, with the seam line lined up with the center point on the open end of the cone. Repeat with 2 more blue-green squares and 5 bright multicolored squares. You'll have a total of 8 tail feathers.

Take 2 multicolored tail feathers and insert the narrow end of feather #1 into the wide opening of feather #2, until the open end point of feather #1 is about 1½ inches from the open end point of feather #2 and the seams on

Fig. 3

the underside of the feathers match. On the seamed side of the 2 feathers, slip stitch the feathers together along the flat-seamed edge of the outer feather to seamed side of the inner feather. Take a blue-green tail feather and slip the narrow end of the two joined multicolor feathers into the blue-green feather so the open end point on the end of the blue-green feather is 1½ inches from the open end point on the top multicolored feather. Slip stitch the flat-seamed edge of the blue-green feather to the seamed side of the multicolored feather. Repeat this step with 2 more multicolored feathers and 1 blue-green feather for 2 sets of tail feathers. (See Fig. 3.)

Place the two sets of tail feathers next to each other, with the seam sides down. Slip stitch the sets of tail feathers together along the inside folded edges of the blue-green feathers only. Place the feathers on the back of the body, with the top / joined point 1 inch away from the back edge of the neck. Slip stitch both outer edges and the point of the blue-green tail feathers to the back of the body.

Take the remaining multi-colored feather and insert it into the remaining blue-green feather until 1½ inches of the inner feather is showing. Slip stitch feathers together on the backside. Center these two feathers on top of the tail feathers on the body until the top blue-green feather point is about ¾ inch farther back toward the bum end than the points of the lower feathers. Slip stitch the outside folded edges of the top blue-green tail feather to the feathers on each side of the tail, starting about 2 inches away from the narrow point, up around the point, and then down 2 inches on the other side.

Step 4. Wings

Take a twill square (see the appendix for instructions for how to weave twill squares) and fold one point down about ½ inch. Fold the square into a triangle shape like you did for the neck, and stitch a ¼-inch seam down one edge from the folded corner to the next point. Turn right side out. Center the seam in the wing like you did for the feathers. Slip stitch the narrow folded corner edge closed. Repeat with the second twill square.

Place the wings on each side of the body, so the fold end is almost

to the front edge of the chest and the top looped edge is next to the outer edge of the tail feathers. Squish the wing sides together a bit to give the wing a little dimension, and slip stitch the top, bottom, and front edges of wing to the body. Leave the back pointed / looped edges of the wing open. Repeat for the wing on the other side of the body.

Step 5. Face

Top knot: Thread a yarn needle with a length of blue-green yarn. Insert the needle into the point on the top of the head and bring the needle tip out about ¼ inch away. Make a loop about 1 inch long and repeat this step in the same spot on the head, for a total of 4 loops. Wrap the yarn around the base of the loops right next to the top of the head, and knot the yarn right next to the top of the head. Push the needle through the head and pull the yarn taut, pulling the knot to the inside of the head. Holding the yarn taut, cut the yarn right where it exits the head. The cut end should go back into the head, and the knot by the loops is hidden.

Eyes: Using the black yarn (or embroidery floss), make a French knot on each side of the head for the eyes.

Switch to white yarn and, using an outline stitch, stitch around the eyes with 2 rows of stitching on the upper side of the eye and 1 row of stitching on the lower side of the eye.

Pablo is ready to strut his stuff!

PROJECT 25
Forsyth the Fox

THE PROJECTS

LIKE ALL FOXES, Forsyth is very pretty and also very smart. The town of Forsyth, Montana, was established in 1876 as the first settlement on the Yellowstone River.

By using the pattern templates in the appendix and playing with the shape of the mouth and length of the eyelashes, you can give Forsyth a delightful personality.

Supplies Needed

96 yards rust DK or light worsted knitting yarn
32 yards black DK or light worsted knitting yarn
32 yards white DK or light worsted knitting yarn
1 yard black fingering weight yarn or embroidery floss for stitching the mouth
Black felt for nose and eyes (template in the appendix)
Stuffing
Black sewing thread and a needle

Weave the squares as follows:

Weave 12 squares of rust yarn
Weave 4 squares of white yarn
Weave 4 squares of black yarn

Refer to "Large Tube" on page 22 for step-by-step photos for constructing the body.

Step 1. Body

Take 2 white squares and lay them on top of each other, matching the corners and edges. On one edge, stitch a ¼-inch seam. Open into rectangle. Set aside. Take 2 rust squares and lay them on top of each other, matching the corners / edges. Stitch a ¼-inch seam on one edge. Open into a rectangle.

You now have 2 rectangles composed of 2 squares each. Lay the rectangles on top of each other, with the right sides together, matching the edges / seam lines / corners. Stitch a ¼-inch seam along both long edges. You now have a tube open on each end, with rust squares on one side and white squares on the other side. The rust squares will be the fox's back, and the white squares are his tummy. Leave the tube wrong side out.

Take another rust square and place it in the opening on one end of the tube, lining up one of the points with a body seam line. Pin the corner so the point sticks up about ½ inch above the edge of the tube opening. Line up the opposite point, with the other body seam line also sticking up about ½ inch above tube edge. Pin. Line up the remaining square points to center between the two pinned points. All four points should stick up about ½ inch above the tube opening edge. Match the edges of the square to the edges of the tube opening, pinning and easing as you go. Now stitch the square into the opening of the tube with a ¼-inch seam, rounding the seam past the points. Turn the body right side out through the opening at the other end of the tube. The tube end with the square sewn in is the fox's bum; the open end will be his neck. Stuff the body firmly so the bum is rounded out slightly. (See Fig. 1.)

Using rust yarn, stitch a running stitch through the loops on the open end of the tube all the way

Fig. 1

129

around the opening, leaving a short tail at the start and finish. Pull the yarn ends tight to close the opening like a drawstring, and tie the yarn in a knot close to the edge of the opening. Trim yarn ends close to the knot. Set the body aside.

Step 2. Head

Muzzle: Take 1 rust square and lay it on top of 1 white square, matching the edges / corners. Starting at a corner, stitch a ¼-inch seam along edge to ½ inch away from the next corner. Stitch straight across this corner and then continue a ¼-inch seam along the next edge, ending seam at the next corner. Two edges of the squares are seamed, and the other two edges are open. (See Fig. 2a.)

Fig. 2a

Fig. 2b

Turn right side out and stuff. The rust square is the top of the head / muzzle. The white square is the chin / neck front. Place the open end of the muzzle on top of the gathered end of the body, so the open point on the white square is centered on the seam line between the white tummy squares. Pin the point. Match the side seams of the muzzle's rust/white squares to the body, with muzzle edges matching the seam lines between white and rust squares on each side of the body. Pin. Slip stitch the bottom edges of the white neck / chin square through the loops to the top white square on the front of the body. Push a little stuffing between the stitched point of the chin and chest on the body. (See Fig. 2b.)

Now place the open point of the rust square over the stuffing at the top of the head, so the edges of this point meet the other edges of the same rust square in a triangle shape on the backside of the head. Slip stitch the looped edges together around this point. (See Fig. 2c.)

Fig. 2c

Fig. 2d

Now you are going to shape the back of the head so it has a nice slope between the top of the head and the body back. Take another rust square and center 1 point at the top of the back of the head. Pin. Center the opposite point of the square at the seamline between the 2 rust squares on the back of the body. Pin. Fold under the points on each side of the square, so the folded edges match the seam line on each side of the body. Pin one side. Place a little stuffing under the square to shape this "back of the neck" square, so it has a nice slope. (See Fig. 2d.) Pin and slip stitch all edges of the square to the backside of the head and body.

After finishing the head, to shape the chin, thread a length of white yarn onto a yarn needle and stitch a short row of running stitch across the front of the neck for about 2 inches, catching a bit of stuffing with each stitch. Pull the yarn tight to make an indent for a bend in the neck.

Ears: Take another rust square and fold into triangle. Fold the triangle in half to make a smaller triangle, with all the looped edges together.

THE PROJECTS

Fig. 2e

Fig. 2f

Fig. 2g

Whip stitch the looped edges together through the loops. The looped edge is the bottom of the ear. Slip stitch the folded edges of the ear together.

Now fold the ear in half, matching looped edges, and make a pleat by stitching ¼ inch away from the folded edge of the pleat for ½ inch through all layers of the ear. (See Fig. 2e.) Open and repeat for the second ear. (See Fig. 2f.)

Place the ears on each side of the head, so the looped edge of the ear matches the edge of the point of the square that was added over the top of the head, the outside point of the ear matches the seam line between the rust and white squares of the muzzle on the sides, and the inside ends of the ears are in the center of the top of the head. Slip stitch the bottoms of the ears to the top of the head around all edges at the bottom of the ears. (See Fig. 2g.)

Step 3. Legs

Front legs: Take 1 black and 1 rust square and lay them on top of each other, matching the edges and points. Stitch a ¼-inch seam on one edge. Repeat with 2 more squares for the second front leg. You have 2 rectangles, each consisting of 1 rust and 1 black square.

Take 1 of the rectangles and fold it in half the long way, with the right sides together, so the rust square edge matches to rust and the black edge matches to black. Starting at the matched corners of the rust square, stitch a ¼-inch seam down the long edge and then across the short edge on the black square end of the rectangle. Turn right side out and stuff firmly. Using rust yarn, whip stitch the top opening closed, starting from the seam line.

Hold the leg so the long seam is down. With the seam line in back, pinch the bottom (black end) of the leg for 1 inch to make a foot. Slip stitch the edges of the pinched fold together. Repeat the steps for the other front leg.

(Refer to "Basic Legs" on page 19 for step-by-step photos for constructing the legs.)

Back legs: Make 2 more black / rust rectangles like you did for the

Fig. 3a

Fig. 3b

front legs, but stitch the seam on the long edge only. Leave the back leg wrong side out and fold back the black end of the leg to the outside, until the black part of the leg measures

131

2 inches from the seam line between the squares to the fold edge. (See Fig. 3a.) Stitch a running stitch in the edge of the fold all the way around the opening, leaving a short beginning tail. Pull running stitch yarn tight like a drawstring to close the opening, and knot the stitching yarn ends close to the fold. Trim yarn ends close to the knot. Turn the leg right side out. Stuff the leg. Whip stitch the open rust end closed from the seam line to the outside edge. Hold the leg with the seam side toward you and fold the leg about 1 inch away from the flat end, so the seam lines on the leg meet. (See Fig. 3b.) Slip stitch edges of the fold together. Repeat for the second back leg.

Placing the legs: Place a back leg on the bottom of the body, so the leg end seam edge is at the seam line between the bum and body back and the bend in the back leg is up. Slip stitch all back-leg edges to the body where they touch. Repeat for the other back leg.

Place the front legs so the seam line of the leg is toward the fox's back and the top edge of the leg matches the bottom seam line of the square that was placed over the back of the neck. Slip stitch all edges of the leg to the body where they touch. Repeat steps for the other front leg.

Step 4. Tail

Take the remaining rust square, fold it in half, and stitch a ¼-inch seam on the long edge only. Turn right side out and stuff into a tube shape.

Tail tip: Take the last white square and fold in thirds. Slip stitch the looped edge to the fold edge on the long edge only. Tightly roll the white tail tip from a narrow end until you reach the other end. Slip stitch the end to the rolled part. Place one rolled side of the tail tip into an end of the rust tail tube, so the seam on the tail tip and tail tube match. Using white yarn, slip stitch the edge of the tail tip to the loops on the end of the stuffed rust part of the tail. On the other end of the tail tip, slip stitch the folded edges on the white tail tip together with white yarn all the way around the tail tip. Center the open end of the tail on the back of the body, so the bottom edge of the tail is about the same level as the bum. Slip stitch the end of the tail to the body around the open end of the tail.

Step 5. Face

Cut 2 eyes and 1 nose out of black felt, using the pattern templates in the appendix. Place the eyes on each side of the head, just below the ears. Slip stitch the edges of the eyes to the head, using sewing thread.

Place the nose on the tip of the muzzle and slip stitch the edges of nose to the muzzle, using sewing thread.

Use the black fingering weight yarn to stitch the mouth, using an outline stitch or split stitch. To make the eyelashes, thread black yarn onto yarn needle and tie a knot ½ inch from the end. Insert the point of the yarn needle into the head just above one eye, and push the needle point through the head so it exits just above the opposite eye. Pull the yarn through until the first knot is snug against the head. Tie another knot in the yarn and tighten the knot so it is right next to the head above the second eye. Cut the yarn with a ½-inch tail. Unply the yarn ends. Trim the eyelashes to your desired length.

Find Forsyth a lovely den to live in!

THE PROJECTS

133

PROJECT 26
Gardiner the Grizzly Bear

THE PROJECTS

GARDINER THE GRIZZLY and Bridger the Bison (see page 138) both celebrate these iconic animals of Yellowstone National Park. Yellowstone Park lies in Wyoming, but the west and north entrances to the park are in Montana. Gardiner is the community at the North Entrance of Yellowstone Park, marked by the famous Roosevelt Arch.

If you'd like to give Gardiner eyes, French knots sewn on each side of the head below the ears, using black knitting yarn or embroidery floss, would work nicely.

Supplies Needed
128 yards brown DK or light worsted knitting yarn
Stuffing

Weave the squares as follows:
16 squares of brown yarn

Refer to "Rounded Body" on page 18 for step-by-step photos for constructing the body.

Step 1. Body

Take 2 squares and lay them on top of each other, matching the corners and edges. Stitch a ¼-inch seam on one edge. Open. You have a rectangle consisting of 2 squares. Repeat with 2 more squares. You now have 2 rectangles consisting of 2 squares each. Lay the rectangles on top of each other, with right sides together, matching edges, corners, and seam lines. Stitch a ¼-inch seam along one long edge. Open. You now have a larger square consisting of 4 small squares.

Take 4 more squares and stitch them together in the same configuration as the first large square. You now have 2 large squares.

Lay one of the large squares on a flat surface, with the right side up. Lay the second large square in a diamond shape on top of first square, with right side down, so the right sides of the squares are together, matching the four corners of the top square to the seam lines on the bottom square. The tips of the corners should be even with the edges of the bottom square. Pin the corners. Now pin the corners of the bottom square to the seam lines of the top square. Match and pin the edges of the two squares between the pinned points. Stitch a ¼-inch seam all the way around the squares, stopping about 1½ inches away from where you started stitching the seam to make an opening for turning / stuffing the body.

Turn the body through the seam opening so the right sides are out. Stuff the body to your desired firmness, shaping the body into an oval shape, with the side-to-side dimensions of the body being a bit narrower than the top-to-bottom dimensions. The seam lines on the body back will be on the bias and look like diamond shapes. The seam lines on the belly side of the body form squares. Turn the edges of the seam opening under and slip stitch the seam opening closed. Set aside.

Step 2. Neck

Take another square and turn under 1 point so it measures 1 inch from the point to the fold. Tack down the corner with a couple of slip stitches. Repeat the process with a second square. The side with the folded points showing is the wrong side of the square. (See Fig. 2.)

Fig. 2

135

Lay the 2 squares on top of each other, with the right sides together, matching the folded edges, looped edges, and points. Starting at one side of the folded-under points edge, stitch a ¼-inch seam from the fold to the first point. On the other side of the folded points, stitch a ¼-inch seam from the fold to the first point on this edge. Turn right side out so the folded points are in the inside. The smaller opening with the folded-back points is the top of the neck where the head will be attached. The larger opening is the body end of the neck.

Place the large opening of the neck over one end of the body, so the top point of the neck opening is centered on the back of the body and the neck point edges match the seam line intersection of the body squares. Pin. Place the opposite point of the neck on the belly, so it matches the seam line running the length of the belly. Pin the point. The seam lines on the neck will be on each side of the body. Pin the remaining sides of the neck so they lie flat against the body, and slip stitch through the loops the edges of the lower neck opening to the front of the body. Stuff the neck firmly between the body and neck, adding extra stuffing under the top side of the neck so Gardiner has a bit of a grizzly shoulder hump. Finish stuffing the neck all the way to the folded edges of the upper end of the neck. Set the body aside.

Step 3. Head

Take 1 square and fold back opposite corners 1 inch. (See Fig. 3a.) Pin the points. Fold the top corner down between the 2 folded points, so that the edges of the top point meet the upper edges of the folded-over points on each side. (See Fig. 3b.) The shape will resemble home plate in baseball. The outside corners between the top flap and side flaps will be the ears. Make a couple of stitches connecting the looped edge of the side point to the looped edge of the top point on each side, starting about ½ inch from the top end of the ears to hold them in place when adding the front of the head. This piece is the back of the bear's head, and the side with the folded-over points showing is the wrong side.

Lay the folded square on flat surface, so the side with the folded points is down. Lay a second square, which will be the front of the head, on top of the first square in a diamond shape, with one point centered between the ears and

Fig. 3a

Fig. 3b

Fig. 3c

Fig. 3d

Fig. 3e

the opposite point on the square matching the bottom point of home plate. Pin the points. Match the points on each side of the top square with the bottom of the outside edges of the ears, one on each side of the flat top of home plate. Pin the points. Match and pin the edges of the squares, from an ear to the middle bottom point and back up to the ear on the other side of the head. Starting from one ear bottom edge, stitch a ¼-inch seam around edges from ear to ear, leaving the top point between the ears open. The top square will not lie flat against the bottom ear square. (See Figs. 3c and 3d.) Turn the head right side out through the opening between the ears. The pleated side of the ears will now face the front of head, and the folded over points will be inside the head. Stuff the head firmly through the opening between the ears into a pear shape. Now fold the front top point between the ears back over the top of the head between the ears until the flap covers the stuffing, and then turn the point of the flap under to the wrong side, so the fold edge matches the folded edge between the ears on the back of the head. Adjust the stuffing if necessary, then slip stitch the folded edges together between the ears. (See Fig. 3e.)

Place the backside of the head on the neck opening, so the top of the head matches the top edge of the neck opening. Slip stitch the backside of the head to the neck opening around all edges of the opening.

Step 4. Legs

Fold 1 of the remaining squares in half. Stitch a ¼-inch seam across one short edge and then continue seam along the long looped edge. Turn right side out and stuff firmly. Hold the looped edges of the opening together, so the seam is on one side, and slip stitch through the loops from seam out to opposite side of the leg to close the top of the leg. Repeat with 3 more squares.

(Refer to "Basic Legs" on page 19 for step-by-step photos for constructing the legs.)

Shape the feet: Holding a leg so the seam line is at the backside of the leg, pinch the end of the leg to create a foot about 1 inch long. Make a couple of stitches through all layers of the fabric and stuffing at the fold, knotting the stitching yarn on the bottom side of the foot. Repeat for the other 3 legs.

Position the legs on the body, with the front legs centered on the lower body seam connecting the neck edge / body, and so the back edges of the back legs are about even with the end of the bum. Pin the tops of the legs to the body to make sure all the legs are the same length. Slip stitch the edges of the legs to the body where leg edges and body touch.

Take Gardiner out for a walk in the woods!

PROJECT 27
Bridger the Bison

WHEN YOU VISIT Yellowstone National Park, you *will* see an American bison, also known as buffalo. Bridger the Bison is named for the small town of Bridger, Montana, which was named for famed mountain man / scout Jim Bridger.

Bridger features a "cape" on his shoulders, giving him that unique bison look.

Supplies Needed

- 100 yards of dark brown DK or light worsted knitting yarn
- 20 yards of black DK or light worsted knitting yarn
- 20 yards of golden brown knitting yarn *or* bumpy textured yarn for the cape
- Stuffing
- 1-inch-wide ruler or piece of cardboard for cape pom-poms

Weave the squares as follows:

- 12 squares of dark brown yarn for body / legs
- 2 squares of black yarn for head

Step 1. Body

Take 2 brown squares and lay them on top of each other, matching the edges / corners. Stitch a ¼-inch seam along one edge. Open. Now lay another square over one of the end squares, matching the corners / edge. Stitch a ¼-inch seam on outside end edge. Open. You now have a rectangle 3 squares long and 1 square high.

Take 2 brown squares and lay them on top of each other, matching the edges / corners. Stitch a ¼-inch seam along one edge. Open. Now lay another square over one of the end squares, matching the corner / edge. Stitch a ¼-inch seam on outside end edges. Open. Lay another square on one end square and stitch a ¼-inch seam on outside end edge. Open. You now have a second rectangle 4 squares long and 1 square high.

Take the 4-square rectangle and lay it right side up on a flat surface. Lay the 3-square rectangle on top of the long rectangle, with right side down, so the right sides of the rectangles are together, matching the center seam on the large 4-square rectangle with the center of the middle square on the 3-square rectangle. Stitch a ¼-inch seam along one long edge. (See Fig. 1a.)

Fold the joined rectangles in half the long way, using the center seam line on the long rectangle as the fold line, so the longer rectangle squares are on top of each other and the short rectangle squares are on top of each other, matching edges all the way around. Starting at the fold in the shorter rectangle, stitch a ¼-inch seam from fold to first corner, then across the bottom edge of the same square to the seam between the 2 rectangles. (See Fig. 1b.) At that seam line, curve the seam you are stitching around the lower corner of the large rectangle, so the stitching line is about 1 inch away from the point.

Fig. 1a

Fig. 1b

Then continue curved seam to the bottom edge of the large rectangle and complete a ¼-inch seam to the outer edge. Leave the body with the wrong side out.

Now take another square and place it inside the large opening on the body, so the right sides are together. This large opening is the chest. Match each corner of the square to the seam lines around the opening, and pin the corners even with the edges of the body / chest opening. Now pin the edges of the square to the edges of the body / chest opening between the pinned points. Stitch a ¼-inch seam around the chest square / body opening, leaving a small opening between the start and end of the seam to turn / stuff the body. Turn the body right side out through the seam opening and stuff the body firmly, shaping it as you go. (See Figs. 1c and 1d.) Turn under the edges of the seam opening and slip stitch the seam opening closed. Set the body aside.

Step 2. Head

Take 2 black squares and lay them on top of each other, matching the points / edges. Starting at one point, stitch a ¼-inch seam from the point along the adjacent edge, around the next point, continue along the next edge, and end the seam at the point across from the point where you started the seam. (See Fig. 2a.) Turn right side out. Stuff the stitched point firmly (this is the nose end of the head) up to the top of the open edges.

Hold the head so you are looking down on the open end. Fold the back point forward over the stuffing and then fold the front point over the top of the stuffing, so the back / front points overlap about ½ to ¾ inch. (See Fig. 2b.) Slip stitch the front point to the back point through the loops on the front point. The openings on each side are for the ears.

In the openings that will be the ears, push the stuffing toward the center of the head. Place the looped edges of one of the ear openings on top of each other and slip stitch the edges together through the loops, starting at the point. When you reach the bottom of the ear, wrap the yarn several times around the bottom of the stitched point, then knot the yarn. On the opposite ear opening, push the stuffing toward the center of the head and add any extra stuffing necessary to get the top of the head to hump upward. Stitch the edges of the second ear together through the loops, starting at the

Fig. 1c

Fig. 1d

Fig. 2a

Fig. 2b

Fig. 2c

tip and ending when you reach the end of the ear opening. (See Fig. 2c.) Wrap yarn several times around base of the ear and knot. Set the head aside.

Step 3. Legs

(Refer to "Cone" on page 21 for step-by-step photos for constructing the legs.)

Take 1 brown square and fold it into a triangle. Stitch a ¼-inch seam along one edge from point to the fold. Turn right side out and stuff firmly all the way to the top of the opening into a cone shape. This is one leg. Repeat for 3 more legs.

Back legs: Place the open end of the back legs so the top of the leg seam matches the seam line on the bottom of the body. Pin. Place the top point of the leg opening so it is about halfway up the side of the bum end of the body and the outer edge of the leg opening is about even with the back seam on the bum. Pin the leg-opening edges, redistributing or adding stuffing so that the upper leg is completely, firmly stuffed between top of the leg and body. Slip stitch the looped edges of the leg opening to the body, all around the leg opening. Repeat for other back leg, checking to make sure the legs are the same length. (Refer to the main project photo of Bridger for leg placement.)

Front legs: Position the front legs so the leg seam is against the side of the body and the point on the leg opening is a little forward from the seam line between the body and chest. Pin the top of the leg edges to the body, confirming that the front leg is the same length as the back legs, and slip stitch through the loops all around the top of the leg to the body. Before you completely close the seam, check the stuffing between the top of the leg and body. Repeat steps for the other front leg.

Refer to main project photo for placement of the head and cape on the body.

Step 4. Placing the Head

Center the head on the chest so the top of the head is slightly below the upper seam line between the chest and body. Slip stitch the back of the head to the chest where the back of the head touches the chest.

Step 5. Cape

Out of either smooth yarn or lumpy textured yarn (both work nicely), depending on what you prefer, make 30 pom-poms. To make the pom-poms, wrap the yarn around a 1-inch-wide ruler or piece of cardboard for 10 wraps, ending on the same side as the starting end of the yarn. Thread a yarn needle with a length of the yarn used for body squares. Slip the needle under the yarn wraps on the ruler, pull the yarn through, and pull to the side with the cut ends. Tie yarn tightly around the yarn wraps, making sure to catch the cut ends, and knot the yarn. Trim the yarn close to the knot and slip the pom-pom off the ruler. Do not cut the loops of the pom-pom!

Place the pom-poms on the sides, back, and chest of the bison, spacing them about ½ to ¾ inch apart, stitching the tie end of the pom-poms to the body. Spread the pom-pom loops out and tack stitch the loops down at whatever interval works to completely cover the shoulders, chest, and front half of the body with the loops.

Step 6. Top Knot and Tail

Top knot: Using the black yarn left over from weaving the head squares, make a pom-pom by wrapping the yarn 20 times around a 1-inch-wide ruler or cardboard. Tie the bottom of the pom-pom with a length of black yarn and cut the loops on the opposite end of the pom-pom. Unravel the plies of each length of yarn. Place the tied end of the top knot pom-pom on the top of the head between the ears, and stitch to the top of the head. Arrange the unplied yarn lengths over the forehead and beside the ears.

Tail: Cut a 6-inch length of the brown body yarn. Fold in half and tie an overhand knot on the folded end. Now twist each of the lengths individually, then put them side by side, tie an overhand knot on the cut ends about 1 inch from the first knot, and let the ends go. The two ends will twist together. Place the knot of the folded end on the top edge of the bum and stitch to body. Trim the cut ends close to the knot.

Bridger is ready to join your herd of Critters!

PROJECT 28
Teton the Teddy Bear

THE PROJECTS

THE SMALLER CRITTERS are cute, but sometimes you just need a big, snuggle-ready Critter to sleep with! Being so much bigger than other Critters, at 12 inches tall seated, Teton is named after a county rather than a town. Teton County is in northwestern Montana on the Rocky Mountain Front. Under the definition of "frontier," which is based on population density of fewer than 7 people per square mile, Teton County is one of 46 counties (out of 56 total) in Montana that are considered frontier.

Supplies Needed

350 yards of brown DK or light worsted knitting yarn

50 yards of rust DK or light worsted knitting yarn

2 yards of black fingering weight yarn or embroidery floss for the face

Black felt for eyes and nose (pattern template for eyes and nose in appendix)

Stuffing

Black sewing thread and needle to attach eyes / nose to face

Weave the squares as follows:

40 squares of brown yarn

6 squares of rust yarn (for paw pads and muzzle)

Sweater supplies: Teton's sweater is sized for a 0–3-month-old baby, so the baby can wear the sweater for a month (or maybe less—babies grow fast), then Teton can wear it! You need one 250-yard skein of worsted weight knitting yarn to knit the sweater, 3 buttons, and size 6 knitting needles.

Refer to the "Rounded Body" on page 18 for step-by-step photos for constructing the body and head. The body and head are assembled using the same steps—only the number of squares used is different!

Step 1. Body

Take 2 brown squares and lay them on top of each other, matching the corners and edges. Stitch a ¼-inch seam along one edge. Open so the right side is up. Lay another square on top of one of the squares, matching the outside edges / corners. Stitch a ¼-inch seam on outside end edge. Open. You now have a rectangle composed of 3 squares across. Repeat to make 2 more sets of rectangles composed of 3 squares each. You have a total of 3 rectangles.

Lay 2 rectangles on top of each other, with right sides together, matching the seam lines, edges, and corners. Stitch a ¼-inch seam along one long edge. Open. You have a rectangle 3 squares across and 2 squares high. Take the last rectangle and place it right sides together along one edge of the 2-square by 3-square rectangle, matching outside edges, corners, and seam lines. Stitch a ¼-inch seam on the long edge. Open. You now have a large square composed of 3 squares across and 3 squares high.

Repeat these steps to make another large square that is 3 squares across by 3 squares high. These 2 large squares are Teton's body. These squares are sewn together like Twodot the Turtle's body, only on a larger scale.

Lay one large square (Teton's back) on a flat surface, with the right side up. Rotate the other large square (Teton's belly) so it is a diamond shape. Lay the belly square right side down on top of the back square, matching one of the outside points of belly square to the center of the edge of the top

143

middle square on the back. Pin the point. Match the opposite point on the belly square to the opposite side of the back square, matching the point to the edge of the center of the middle square. Pin. Now match the corners of the belly square to the center of the edges of the middle square of the large back square on each side.

Now match the 4 points on the back square to the edges of the middle squares on the large belly square and pin. Match the edges of the belly and back squares between the pinned points, pinning the edges as you go. Stitch a ¼-inch seam around all pinned edges of the body, leaving a small opening between the start and end of the seam to turn / stuff the body.

Turn the body right side out through the seam opening. Stuff the body to desired firmness and shape the body so it is a rectangular shape, with the squares on the bias being the belly side and the side with the squares straight across is the back. Turn the edges of the seam opening under and slip stitch the opening closed. Set the body aside.

Step 2. Head

The head is made like the body, but the front and back of the head are 2 large squares composed of 4 small squares, each out of the brown yarn.

Take 2 brown squares and lay them on top of each other, matching the corners / edges. Stitch a ¼-inch seam on one edge. Open into rectangle. Repeat with 2 more small squares. You have 2 rectangles composed of 2 squares each.

Lay one rectangle on flat surface, with the right side up. Lay the second rectangle on top, with the right side down, matching the seam lines, edges, and corners. Stitch a ¼-inch seam along one long edge. Open. You have a square consisting of 4 small squares. Set it aside. Repeat the steps with another 4 squares. You have 2 squares each composed of 4 small squares.

Lay the first square on a flat surface, with the right side up. Lay the second square on top, with the right side down in a diamond shape, matching the top point to the edge of the bottom square at the seam line between the squares. Pin. Match the opposite point of the top square to the edge / seam line on the bottom square. Pin. Match the remaining top side points to the seam lines on the bottom square on each side. Pin. Now match the points of the bottom square to the seam lines on the top square and pin the points. Match the edges of the top and bottom squares between the pinned points, pinning as you go. Stitch a ¼-inch seam around all the edges, leaving a small opening between the beginning and end of the seam.

Turn the head right side out through the seam opening and stuff it into a round shape. Turn the edges of the seam opening under, and slip stitch the seam opening closed. The face side is where the seams are on the bias, and the backside of the head is where the seams go straight across. Set the head aside.

Step 3. Ears

Take one of the brown squares and fold it into a triangle. Whip stitch through the loops along the looped edges. Fold the triangle in half to make a smaller triangle, matching the looped edges. (See Fig. 3a.) On the fold side, stitch a ¼-inch seam for ½ inch to create a pleat. (See Fig. 3b.) Open the triangle. Repeat with another brown square for the other ear. Set the ears aside.

Fig. 3a

Fig. 3b

Step 4. Muzzle

Take 2 of the rust squares and lay them on top of each other, match-

Fig. 4

ing the corners / edges. Stitch a ¼-inch seam starting at one point, along the edge, and stopping ¾ inch away from the next point. Stitch straight across the second point, ¾ inch away from the point, then continue a ¼-inch seam along the next edge. You will have a seam along 2 edges and no seam on the opposite edges. (See Fig. 4.) Turn the muzzle right side out and stuff.

Step 5. Assembling the Face

The side of the head with the squares on bias is the face side of the head. Place the ears on each side of the top of the head, lining up the pleat in the ear with the seam line on the face. Slip stitch the bottom edge of the ears to the head.

Hold the stuffed muzzle so the seam lines are on the sides. Turn the unstitched top corner back over the stuffing about 1 inch. Place the muzzle on the face so the fold line is at the center of the face and the lower point on the opposite side from the fold is at the neck end of the head. Pin the edges of the muzzle to the head. Once you are pleased with the muzzle placement, slip stitch through the loops the edges of the muzzle to the head around all muzzle edges, adjusting the stuffing as necessary.

Using the pattern template in the appendix, cut 2 eyes and a nose out of black felt. Place the eyes on each side of the muzzle and place the nose on the front of the muzzle. Pin and check that you like the placement. Slip stitch the eyes and nose edges to the head, using black sewing thread / needle.

Place the head on top of the body so the body belly seams on the bias are on the same side as the face. Slip stitch the bottom edges of the head to the top of the body all the way around the bottom of the head. I suggest doing 2 or 3 rows of stitching around the head, starting from the inner edges to outer edges to make the head secure and so that it doesn't flop forward as easily. Set the body aside.

Step 6. Arms and Legs

Arms: Take 2 brown squares and lay them on top of each other, matching the corners and edges. Stitch a ¼-inch seam on one edge. Open. Repeat with 1 brown square and 1 rust square. You have 2 rectangles composed of 2 squares each. Lay the rectangles on top of each other, with the right sides together. Stitch a ¼-inch seam starting at the end corner where the 2 brown squares are on top of each other along the long edge, then across the short edge rounding past the corners on each side, and continue seam down the opposite long edge. (See Fig. 6a.) Turn right side out through the end opening. Stuff the arm and slip stitch the open end closed from seam line to seam line. (See Fig. 6b.) The rust square is the "paw pad" and is on the front inside edge of the arm when you place it on the body. Repeat for the second arm.

Place arms on each side of the upper body so the sides of the arms with the rust paw pad are facing toward each other across the belly. Slip stitch the tops of the arms to the shoulders of the upper body, with the arms sticking out toward the sides.

Legs: Make 2 legs just like the 2 arms. The rust squares will now be the bottom of the feet. Lay the stuffed legs on a flat surface, so

Fig. 6a

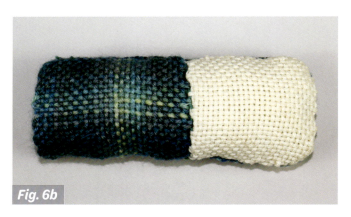
Fig. 6b

Fig. 6c

you are looking at the side with 2 brown squares and the end with the rust square is toward you on the bottom side of the leg. Fold the foot back at the seam line between the brown and rust squares. Now the rust square is the bottom of the foot. Slip stitch the edges of the fold together so the foot sticks up. (See Fig. 6c.)

Place the legs on each side of the bottom of the body so the feet are facing up. Slip stitch the edges of the legs to the bottom of the body. Refer to the main project photo for leg placement.

Step 7. Mouth

Using black fingering weight yarn or embroidery floss, stitch Teton's mouth . If you don't want to make Teton a sweater, you are done! Read on if you want to knit him a sweater.

TETON THE TEDDY'S SWEATER

Custom-designed for Teton by Diana McKay, retired owner of Mountain Colors Yarns

Yarn: 250-yard skein of worsted weight knitting yarn

Needles: #6 US circular or straight needles

Gauge: 4.5 stitches = 1 inch

Size: 0–3 months

Abbreviations:
K = Knit
P = Purl
YO = Yarn Over
K2TOG = Knit 2 stitches together

The sweater is knit all in one piece, starting from the back bottom edge and then seamed together at the sides / underarms of sleeves.

Back: Cast on 46 stitches. Work K1, P1 Rib for 1 inch. Knit 1 row, increasing 6 stitches evenly across row. (52 stitches total) Work stockinette stitch (Knit on right side, Purl back on wrong side) until the back measures 5 inches from cast on row. End on a purl row.

Sleeves: Cast on 18 stitches for the sleeves at the start of the next two rows. (88 stitches total)

Work stockinette stitch for 4 inches while working K4 Border on every row. End after a purl row.

Split for neck / continue sleeve on one side

You will work on one side of the front at a time from this point. Knit across 31 stitches. Place the next 57 stitches on a stitch holder or another needle to be worked later. Purl back 31 stitches.

***Work stockinette stitch with established edge stitches and increase 1 stitch every other row at the neck edge. Continue until sleeve measures about 8 inches total and you have 40 stitches. End after a purl row.

Sweater front panels: Starting at the sleeve cuff edge, bind off 18 stitches. Work stockinette stitch on remaining 22 stitches until 4 inches from sleeve bind off. K1, P1 Rib for 1 inch. Bind off loosely.

Go back to the stitches on the holder. Keep the 26 center stitches on the holder for the sweater neck. You will work the remaining 31 stitches the same as for the first sleeve. Go to *** and repeat this section and the front panel section for the second side of the sweater.

Finishing: Block the sweater by soaking in warm water and laying flat to dry. Sew the underarm seams.

Button band: Starting at the bottom right front edge and moving up, pick up 18 band stitches along the front-edge place marker. When you reach the "V" edge, pick up 15 collar stitches to the back-neck place marker. You will now knit the 26 neck stitches that are still on the holder place marker. Now move down the other side, picking up 15 collar stitches to the "V" place marker, and then pick up 18 band stitches along the front edge.

Work the edge / button band stitches as follows:

Rows 1, 2, and 3: Work a K1, P1 rib.

Row 4: Space buttonholes as desired and use the following for the holes on the right band edge: YO, K2TOG, K1, P1 Rib.

Row 5: Work one more row of ribbing (K1, P1).

Row 6: Bind off in pattern to the first marker. Stop at the beginning of the "V" and knit the collar stitches, neck stitches, and other side of the collar stitches.

Bind off the second set of band stitches. You now have only the collar, neck, and second side of collar stitches on your needle. You will work stockinette stitch for 4 rows. Bind off loosely on next row.

Introduce your well-dressed bear to a favorite person in your life!

PROJECT 29
Darby the Dog

DARBY THE DOG is 12 inches tall, delightfully floppy, full of personality, and named for the town of Darby in the southern end of the Bitterroot Valley, which happens to be the same mountain valley where I live.

Supplies Needed

300 yards of brown DK or light worsted knitting yarn

32 yards of rust DK or light worsted knitting yarn

1 yard of black fingering weight yarn or embroidery floss

Red and black felt (for the face)

Stuffing

Black sewing thread and needle to sew on the eyes, nose, and tongue

Weave the squares as follows:

37 squares of brown yarn

4 squares of rust yarn

Step 1. Body

Refer to "Large Tube" on page 22 for step-by-step photos for constructing the body.

Take 2 brown squares and lay them on top of each other, matching the corners and edges. Stitch a ¼-inch seam along one edge. Open. You have a rectangle composed of 2 squares. Repeat with another 2 squares.

Place the 2 rectangles on top of each other, with right sides together, matching long edge, middle seam lines, and corners. Stitch a ¼-inch seam along one long edge. Open. You now have a large square consisting of 4 small squares.

Repeat the first two body steps to create a second large square consisting of 4 small squares.

Lay one large square on a flat surface, with the right side up. Lay the second large square on top of the first square, with the right side down, matching the corners, seam lines, and edges. Stitch a ¼-inch seams on the opposite edges of the large squares. You now have a large tube open on top and bottom edges that is 4 squares around and 2 squares high. Leave the tube wrong side out.

Take another brown square and place it inside an open end of the tube, matching the small square's points to the tube edges at the seam lines of the tube. Pin the points. Now match and pin the edges of square to the edges of the tube around the opening. Stitch a ¼-inch seam all around the square / tube opening. Turn right side out and stuff firmly.

The open end is the neck end of the body, and the closed end is Darby's bum. Stitch a running stitch around the neck opening about a ¼ inch from the edges of the opening, leaving a 2-inch tail at the beginning and end of the stitching. Pull on the stitching yarn tails like a drawstring to close the top of the body until the opening is about 1½ inches across. Tie a knot in the stitching yarn and trim the yarn tails close to the knot. Set the body aside.

Step 2. Neck

Take 2 more brown squares and fold down one corner on each square 1½ inches measured from point to fold. The side where you see only the edge of the fold is the right side. Lay the squares on top of each other, with the right sides together, matching the folded edges and the corners / edges next to the folds. Pin. On each side of the folded edges, stitch ¼-inch seams from the folds to the first point. Turn the neck right side out so the folded-back points are now on the inside of the neck. (See Fig. 2.) The opening with the folded edges is the top of the neck. The larger opening becomes the shoulders / bottom of neck. Put a bit of stuffing in the top end of the neck.

Place the large opening of the neck over the top of the body, so the bottom neck points match the center front and center back seam lines on the body and are about 1 inch above the seam line that runs horizontally around the body. Pin the points. Match the seam lines on the sides of the neck to the seam lines on the left and right sides of the body, so the ends of the seams on the lower edge of the neck are 2½ inches above the seam running horizontally around the body. Pin the sides. Pin the looped edges of the lower neck so the edges lie smoothly around the body, and slip stitch through the loops the lower neck edge to the body. Add stuffing through the top neck opening to shape the neck into the shoulders / neck. Set the body aside.

Step 3. Head

(Refer to "Small Closed Body Tube" on page 20 for step-by-step photos for constructing the head.)

Take 2 more brown squares and lay them on top of each other, matching the corners and edges. Stitch a ¼-inch seam on one edge. Open. Place another brown square on one of the squares, matching the outer corners and edge. Stitch a ¼-inch seam on the outer end edge. Open into a rectangle 3 squares long by 1 square high. Fold the rectangle in half the long way, with the right sides together, matching the edges and corners of the single squares on each end of the rectangle. Pin the outside edges of the end squares together and stitch a ¼-inch seam. You now have a tube that is 3 squares around and 1 square high. Leave the head tube wrong side out.

Top and bottom of head: Place another brown square in an open end of the tube, so the right sides are together and one point of the square is centered on the edge of one of the tube squares. This is the front of the head. Pin. Match the opposite point of the square to the seam line of the tube opposite the first pinned point. Pin the point. This point is at the back of the head. Center the remaining points to opposite sides of the tube opening between the pinned points. Pin the points and then match / pin the edges of the square to the edges of the head tube. Stitch a ¼-inch seam around the top of the head.

Repeat these steps with another brown square in the opening on the other end of the tube but leave a small opening between the start and end of the seam. Turn the head right side out through the opening. Stuff the head firmly so the top and bottom squares are rounded out slightly. Turn the edges of the seam opening under and slip stitch the seam opening closed.

(Refer to "Cone" on page 21 for step-by-step photos for constructing the ears.)

Ears: Take a brown square and fold into a triangle. Whip stitch through the loops on one edge from fold to point. Open into a cone shape by lining up the seam line with the open end point. Repeat with another brown square.

Hold the head so a seam line between the squares is at the back of the head. Lay the small point of one of the ears on a side of the

Fig. 2

THE PROJECTS

Fig. 3a

Fig. 3b

head, with the seamline on the ear facing you, the small point of the cone pointing down toward the bottom of the head, and the end of the small point about ½ inch below the seam line around the top of the head. Slip stitch both edges of the small point of the ear to the side of the head, starting and ending at the seam line between the head and top of the head. (See Fig. 3a.) Now fold the ear down toward the bottom of the head and slip stitch the fold on the top edge of the ear to the top of the head. This makes the ears stick out a bit from the sides of the head. (See Fig. 3b.) Repeat to attach the other ear on the opposite side of the head.

Muzzle: Take 2 brown squares and lay them on top of each other, matching the edges / corners. (See Fig. 3c.) Stitch a ¼-inch seam on opposite sides of the squares so you have a tube. Turn right side out. Stuff firmly. With an open end facing you, fold the seamed side edges over until they meet in the middle over the stuffing. (See Fig. 3d.) Now fold the top and bottom edges over until they meet. Pin

Fig. 3c

Fig. 3e

Fig. 3d

and slip stitch all the edges. (See Fig. 3e.) This is the nose end of the muzzle.

On the open end of the muzzle, fold the edge back into the muzzle until the muzzle measures 1½ inches long, removing some stuffing if necessary. Place the open end of the muzzle against the front of the head, so the seams on each side of the muzzle are below the ears and the bottom of the muzzle matches the bottom seam line around the base of the head. Slip stitch around the folded edge of the muzzle to attach the end of the muzzle to the head.

Refer to the main project photo for placement of muzzle, head, neck, and legs.

Place the bottom of the head on top of the neck opening of the body, with the muzzle centered over the center seam line on the body. Slip stitch the neck opening to the bottom of head around the edges. Adjust the stuffing in the neck, if necessary, before you complete the stitching. Set the body aside.

Step 4. Legs

The legs are constructed like Darby's body. Lay two brown squares on top of each other, matching the corners and edges. Stitch a ¼-inch seam along one edge. Open. You have a rectangle of 2 brown squares. Repeat with 2 more brown squares.

Lay the rectangles on top of each other, with the right sides together. Stitch ¼-inch seams on both long edges, leaving both short edges open. You have a tube 2 squares long and 2 squares around. Leave the tube wrong side out.

Place one of the rust squares (these are the paw pads) into one of the openings of the tube, so the right sides are together. Match a corner of the rust square to a seam line on the tube with the point of the square sticking up over the edge of the opening about ½ inch. Match the opposite point on the rust square to the seam line on the opposite side of tube. Pin the remaining points centered in the tube squares. All the rust square points should extend ½ inch above the edges of the opening. Match the tube edges and square edges between the pinned points and stitch a ¼-inch seam around the square / tube opening, rounding the seam past the points. Turn the leg right side out and stuff. Lay the edges of the open end together so the seams are on the sides of the leg, and slip stitch the end opening closed. Repeat for 3 more legs.

Optional: If you'd like to make ankles to define the feet, pinch the leg about an inch above the rust paw pad and make a couple of stitches through both layers of the leg and the stuffing to make an "ankle" in the leg.

Place the bottom legs so the seam on the narrow end of the leg matches the seam line between the bum and body and the legs make a wide "V" shape. Slip stitch the seamed ends of the bottom legs to the body.

Place the seamed end of the upper legs on each side of the upper part of the body by the seamline between the bottom of the neck and the top of the body. Slip stitch only the end of the legs to the body, so the legs are nice and floppy. (Refer to the main project photo for reference.)

Step 5. Tail

Take the last brown square and fold it in half. Whip stitch the long edge through the loops. Knot the stitching yarn. Now stitch a running stitch through the loops on the narrow end and pull the stitching yarn tight like a drawstring to close the end of the tail, and tie a knot. Cut the stitching yarn close to the knot. Turn the tail right side out and stuff the tail firmly through the open end into a half a hot-dog-type shape. Center the open end of the tail on Darby's back, so the bottom edge of the tail is at the seam line between the bum and back. Slip stitch the edges of the end of the tail to the back all the way around the tail opening.

Step 6. Face

Using the pattern templates for the eyes, nose, and tongue in the appendix, cut 2 eyes and the nose out of black felt and the tongue out of red felt. Place the eyes above the muzzle on each side of the head. Slip stitch the edges of the eyes to the head, using black sewing thread. Place the nose on the end of the muzzle and slip stitch the edges of the nose to the muzzle. Place the tongue on the front of the muzzle right below the nose, matching the flat end of the tongue to the bottom edge of the nose. Slip stitch the end of the tongue to the muzzle with red sewing thread. Use the black fingering weight yarn or embroidery floss to stitch eyebrows, using a split stitch.

Give Darby a great big hug!

THE PROJECTS

153

PROJECT 30
Kinsey the Kitty

KINSEY THE KITTY is named for the unincorporated community of Kinsey, located in eastern Montana on the Yellowstone River. This is an area for those who love primitive camping and exploring the great outdoors. Sitting 12 inches tall, Kinsey is for anyone who prefers to snuggle with bigger kitties than Cascade the Cat.

Supplies Needed

220 yards of gray DK or light worsted knitting yarn

120 yards of white DK or light worsted knitting yarn

Bright blue felt (eyes) and pink felt (nose)

Stuffing

White sewing thread and needle

Weave the squares as follows:

27 squares of gray yarn

15 squares of white yarn

Refer to "Large Tube" on page 22 for step-by-step photos for constructing the body.

Step 1. Body

Take 2 gray squares and lay them on top of each other, matching the corners and edges. Stitch a ¼-inch seam along one edge. Open. You have a rectangle 2 squares long and 1 square high. Make 2 more rectangles of 2 gray squares each, for a total of 3 rectangles.

Lay a rectangle on a flat surface, with the right side up. Lay a second rectangle on top, with the right side down, so right sides of the rectangles are together. Stitch a ¼-inch seam along one long edge. Open. Take the 3rd rectangle and lay it right sides together on top of one of the connected rectangles, matching edges and outer corners. Stitch a ¼-inch seam along the long edge. You now have a large rectangle composed of 6 gray squares—3 squares across and 2 squares high.

Take 2 white squares and lay them on top of each other, matching the corners and edges. Stitch a ¼-inch seam on one edge. Open. Lay the 2-square white rectangle on top of a 2-square end of the large gray rectangle, matching the center seam lines, outer corners, and edges. Stitch a ¼-inch seam on the 2 squares edge, only connecting one end of the longer gray rectangle with one edge of the white squares. Open. You have a rectangle 4 squares long (3 gray squares plus 1 white square) and 2 squares high. Lay this new rectangle flat, with the right side up. Now take the opposite end of the rectangle that has 2 gray squares and fold it over to lay on top of the 2 white squares on the other end of the rectangle, matching center seam lines, corners, and edges. Stitch a ¼-inch seam on the edge, connecting 2 gray squares to 2 white squares. You now have a tube 2 squares high and 4 squares around. The stacked white squares are the tummy. The stacked gray squares are the sides and back of the body. Leave the tube with the wrong side out.

Adding the bum: Take another gray square and place it in one of the tube openings, with the right sides together, matching the points on the square with the seam lines on the tube. The points of the square should stick up about ¼ inch above the edge of the tube. Pin all the points. Match and pin the edges of the tube to the edges of the square between the pinned points. Stitch a ¼-inch seam around the edges, rounding slightly past the points.

Turn the body right side out and firmly stuff all the way to the top of the opening. Using gray yarn, stitch a running stitch about ¼ inch from the top edge of the tube opening, leaving a 2-inch tail of yarn at the beginning and end of stitching. Pull on both tails to close the top of the body like a drawstring until the opening is about 1 inch across. Securely knot the stitching yarn and trim the ends close to the knots. Set the body aside.

Step 2. Head

(Refer to "Rounded Body" on page 18 for step-by-step photos for constructing the head.)

Kinsey's head is made just like Teton the Teddy Bear's head and Twodot's body. Take 2 gray squares and lay them on top of each other, matching the corners / edges. Stitch a ¼-inch seam on one edge. Open into a rectangle. Repeat with 2 more gray squares. You have 2 rectangles composed of 2 squares each.

Lay one rectangle on a flat surface, with the right side up. Lay a second rectangle on top, with the right side down, matching seam lines, edges, and corners. Stitch a ¼-inch seam along one long edge. Open. You have a square consisting of 4 small squares. Set aside. Repeat the steps with another 4 squares, so you have 2 large squares each composed of 4 small squares.

Lay the first large square on a flat surface, with the right side up. Lay the second square on top in a diamond shape, with the right side down, matching the end of the top point of the top square to the seam line between two squares on the lower square. Pin. Match the opposite point of the top square to the edge / seam line on that end of the lower square. Pin. Match the remaining top square points to the seam lines on each side of the lower square. Pin. Now match the corners on the lower square to the seam lines on the top square. Pin. Match the edges of the top and lower squares between the pinned points, pinning the edges together as you go. Stitch a ¼-inch seam around all the edges, leaving small opening between the beginning and end of the seam.

Turn the head right side out through the seam opening and stuff the head into a round shape from the front and an oval shape from the side. The face side is where the seam lines are on the bias, and the back of the head is where the seam lines go straight across. Set the head aside.

Fig. 2a

Fig. 2b

Ears: Take a gray square and fold it into a triangle. Whip stitch the looped edges together. Fold the triangle in half to make a smaller triangle, matching the looped edges. (See Fig. 2a.) At the looped edge side of the fold, stitch a ¼-inch seam for ½ inch to create a pleat. Open the triangle. (See Fig. 2b.) The side with the pleat is the backside of the ear. Repeat for the second ear. Set the ears aside.

Nose: Lay 2 white squares on top of each other, matching the corners / edges. Starting at one corner, stitch

Fig. 2c

a ¼-inch seam along one edge until you are 1½ inches away from the next corner. Stitch straight across that corner and then continue a ¼-inch seam down the next edge to the next corner. Your squares are stitched together on 2 edges. (See Fig. 2c.) Turn the right side out and stuff. Set the nose aside.

Refer to the main project photo for head placement on the body, adding the ears and nose to the head.

Step 3. Attach Head to Body

Place the head on the gathered end of the body, so the head seams that are on the bias are above the white squares on the belly. Slip stitch the bottom of the head to the top of the body where the edges touch. I recommend 2-3 rounds of stitches that start close to the center of the bottom of the head and move outward a bit on each round to securely attach the head to the body.

Step 4. Making the Face

Place the ears on each side of the top of the head, with the seam side of the pleat toward the back of the head and centering the front side of the pleat with the seam line on the front of the head. Slip stitch the bottom of the ears to the head.

Take the stuffed nose and lay it on the front of the head, with the seams on the sides of the nose. Place the upper open point so it is centered on the head between the ears. Pin the point. Place the lower open point at the bottom of

the head and fold the bottom point back into the inside of the nose until the fold edge is even with the seam between the head and top of the body. Pin.

Measure down 1½ inches from the top point into the nose and flatten the top point against the head by removing any stuffing behind that top point. Pin this nose point to the head at the 1½-inch measurement from the top point. Pin the edges of the top point to the head. Lay the remaining edges of the nose against the head so the edges lie smoothly, adjusting the nose stuffing as necessary. Slip stitch through the loops all the way around the edges of the nose to the front of the head. With white yarn, stitch a running stitch at the top of the nose through the nose and into the front of the head across the top nose point where you placed the pin 1½ inches from the top point to hold that top nose point flat to the head. Set the body aside.

Step 5. Legs

Upper legs: Take 1 gray square and 1 white square and lay them on top of each other, matching the corners and edges. Stitch a ¼-inch seam along one edge. Open. You have a rectangle composed of 1 gray and 1 white square. (See Fig. 5a.) Repeat with another gray and white square.

Lay one gray/white rectangle on a flat surface, with the right side up. Lay the second gray/white rectangle on top, with the right side down, matching the gray squares and white squares, seam lines, corners, and edges. Pin the edges.

Fig. 5a

Fig. 5b

Starting at the narrow end of the rectangles with the gray squares, stitch a ¼-inch seam down a long edge, then around the seam past the corners on the outside end of the white squares, and continue a ¼-inch seam down the other long edge. Turn the upper leg right side out through the opening at the end with the gray squares. Stuff the leg and slip stitch the opening closed from seam to seam. (See Fig. 5b.) Repeat for the second upper leg.

Attaching the upper legs to the body: Place the gray end of the leg against the body, so the end seam is at an angle against the body and the legs point down and slightly forward. Slip stitch the top of the upper leg to the body where they touch. Repeat for the other upper leg.

Lower legs: Make 2 more gray/white rectangles as you did for the upper legs. Place the rectangles on top of each other, with the right sides together, matching the gray squares and the white squares. Stitch a ¼-inch seam along both long edges, leaving both narrow ends open so you have a tube. Take a white square and place it right sides together in the white-squares end of the tube, matching a point of the square to one of the seam lines. The point should stick up about ½ inch above the edge of the tube opening. Pin. Now match the opposite point to the other seam line and pin. Match the remaining points to the centers of the squares on each side. Pin. All points should stick above the edge of the tube opening about ½ inch. Pin the edges of the tube and squares together between the pinned points around the opening. Stitch a ¼-inch seam around the opening, rounding the seam past the points. This is the bottom of the foot for the lower leg. Turn the leg right side out and stuff firmly. Place the edges of the opening together so the seam lines on the long edges match, and whip stitch through the loops to close the opening. Repeat for the second lower leg.

Place the end seam on the gray end of the leg against the body, so the bottom edge of the leg matches the seam line between the bum and body. Slip stitch the edges of the legs to the body where they touch. Repeat with the other lower leg.

Optional: If you would like to give the lower leg feet some definition, thread some white yarn on your yarn needle. Insert the point of the needle from the front of the leg about 1 inch above the seam line for the leg / bottom of the foot and exit on the backside of the leg at the foot / leg seam on the back of the leg. Move the needle over about ½ inch, insert, and come out through the top of the leg, in line with the first stitch, then send the needle to the backside of the leg again. Pull the yarn tight to make a dent in the leg above the foot. Knot the yarn on the underside of the leg.

Step 6. Tail

Lay the 2 remaining gray squares on top of each other, matching the corners and edges. Stitch a ¼-inch seam along one edge. Open with the right side up. Lay the remaining white square on top of one of the gray squares, matching the edges and corners. Stitch a ¼-inch seam on the outside end edge. You now have a rectangle composed of 2 gray squares and a white square on one end.

Fold the rectangle in half the long way, with the right sides together, matching the edges and seam lines to make a long, skinny rectangle. Starting on the end with the white square, stitch a ¼-inch seam from the fold edge across the narrow end of the skinny rectangle and then continue the seam down the long edge. Turn the tail right side out and stuff the entire tail so that the white end of the tail rounds out a bit at the end seam.

Center the open end of the tail on the back, with the tail seam line down, so that the tail seam line matches the seam line between the bum and body. Slip stitch the edges of the tail end to the body all around the tail end.

Step 7. Face

Using the pattern templates in the appendix, cut 2 eyes out of blue felt and one nose out of pink felt. Place the eyes on the sides of the nose, overlapping the eyes with the edges of the top point. Slip stitch the edges of the eyes to the head, using sewing thread. Place the nose on the end of the white muzzle / nose and slip stitch the edges of the nose to the muzzle.

Using the remaining gray yarn, stitch the mouth under the nose, using a split stitch. For whiskers, thread a needle with about 24 inches of the remaining gray yarn and tie a knot about 2 inches from the end. Enter your needle from one edge of the pink nose and exit on the other edge of the pink nose. Tie a knot in the yarn right next to the nose. Cut a 2-inch tail. Repeat 2 more times for 3 whiskers on each side. Trim the whiskers to your desired length.

To add eyelashes, thread gray yarn onto a yarn needle and tie a knot 1 inch from the end. Enter the needle at the outside edge of the eye and bring the point back up right next to the beginning of the stitch. Pull the yarn through until the knot is at the edge of the eye. Tie another knot in the yarn on the needle and tighten so the knot is right next to the eye. You have 2 eyelashes. Repeat for as many eyelashes as you want on each eye. Trim the eyelashes ½ inch or your desired length.

And Kinsey is ready to snuggle!

Appendix

FACE PATTERNS

A simple approach is to cut the facial features out of felt.

Pryor the Panda: Eyes and Nose

Polaris the Penguin: Eyes

Cascade the Cat and Laurel the Lion: Eyes and Nose

Ovando the Octopus: Eyes

Forsyth the Fox: Eyes and Nose

Teton the Teddy Bear: Eyes and Nose

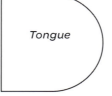

Darby the Dog: Eyes, Nose, and Tongue

Kinsey the Kitty: Eyes and Nose

APPENDIX

WEAVING WITH A DIFFERENT-COLORED YARN

Olney the Owl, Tarkio the T-Rex, Ovando the Octopus, and Pablo the Peacock all have squares that use two different color yarns in one square. You can use this technique for any of the Critters in the book.

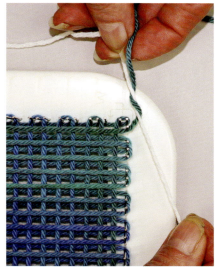

Wind the first three rounds of yarn onto the loom. Tie on the new yarn by wrapping the tail twice around the yarn.

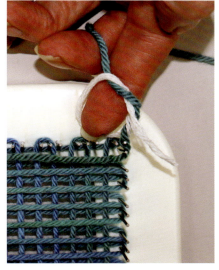

Now make a loop around your finger and insert the tail of the new yarn into the loop.

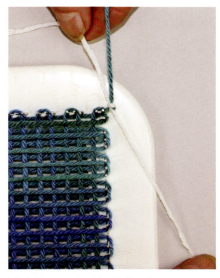

Holding on to the tail of yarn on the loom, pull on the tail of the new yarn to tighten the knot, and slide the knot next to the pins. Cut off the tail of old yarn, wind the new yarn 5 times around the loom, and weave.

Fig. 1

The completed square features spots of the new color. (See Fig. 1.)

To make a striped square, tie on the new yarn color after the second round on the loom. Then wind the third round of yarn onto the loom, using the new color, and weave the square with the new color. (See Fig. 2.)

Fig. 2

163

HOW TO WEAVE TWILL SQUARES

Wind the yarn onto the pin loom as you normally would for the first round. Yarn comes out in the small space between the two pins next to the #2. (See Fig. 1.)

Holding onto the yarn, turn the loom 180 degrees so the corner you just exited is at the upper left corner now. Wrap the yarn around the one pin to the right, then continue winding the yarn around 2 pins across the loom as you normally would. The yarns of the second layer will lie between the yarns of the first layer. (See Fig. 2.)

Tie on the multicolored yarn and wind it around the loom eight times. Start weaving on the lower right-hand corner of the loom, wrapping the yarn around one pin on each side when you start weaving a new row, with one pin between the end of the row and start of the next row. There will be times when there is not a pin, but rather the larger space between sets of pins. This space counts as a "pin." Simply weave across in the space and snug your yarn up to the first warp thread when you pull the weaving yarn through. (See Fig. 3.)

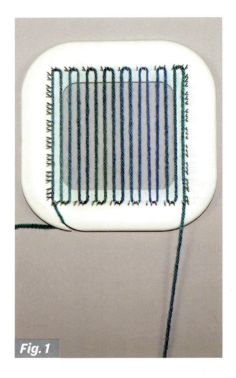
Fig. 1

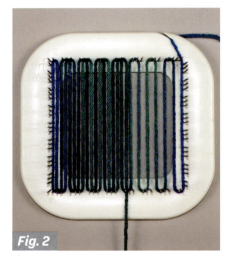
Fig. 2

You may want to weave a "learning square" the first time.

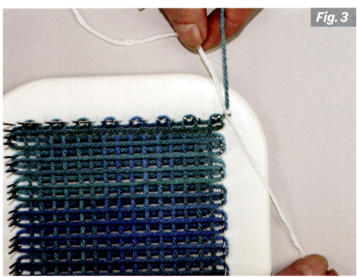
Fig. 3

164

APPENDIX

Twill on Two Layers

NOTE: When weaving, go around only 1 pin at the sides, leaving only 1 open pin or space between picks. Reference: *100 Pin Loom Squares*, by Florencia Campos Correa, pages 39-44; Quantum Books, 2015, St. Martin's Griffin Press

Abbreviations:
U means the tip of your weaving needle goes UNDER threads on the loom.

O means the tip of your weaving needle goes OVER threads on the loom.

"Weave Across" means you weave over / under across the row

Instructions in parenthesis are woven as a repeated *unit* across the row. Example: (O2: U2) is a repeated unit where your needle tip goes Over 2 threads then Under 2 threads across the row.

Row 1: Start U1 and Weave across.
Row 2: (O2; U2) Repeat to end; U1
Row 3: (O2, U2) Repeat to end; U1
Row 4: O1; U1; (O2, U2) Repeat to end; O1
Row 5: (U2; O2) Repeat to end; O1
Row 6: U1; O1; (U2; O2) Repeat to end; U1
Row 7: (O2; U2) Repeat to end; U1
Row 8: O1; U1; (O2; U2) Repeat to end; O1
Row 9: (U2; O2) Repeat to end; O1
Row 10: U1; O1; (U2, O2) Repeat to end; U1
Row 11: (O2; U2) Repeat to end; U1
Row 12: O1; U1; (O2; U2) Repeat to end; O1
Row 13: (U2; O2) Repeat to end; O1
Row 14: U1; O1; (U2; O2) Repeat to end; U1
Row 15: (O2; U2) Repeat to end; U1
Row 16: O1; U1; (O2; U2) Repeat to end; O1
Row 17: (U2; O2) Repeat to end; O1
Row 18: U1; O1; (U2; O2) Repeat to end; U1
Row 19: (O2; U2) Repeat to end; U1
Row 20: O1; U1; (O2; U2) Repeat to end; O1
Row 21: (U2; O2) Repeat to end; O1
Row 22: U1; O1; (U2; O2) Repeat to end; U1
Row 23: (O2; U2) Repeat to end; U1
Row 24: O1; U1; (O2; U2) Repeat to end; O1
Row 25: (U2; O2) Repeat to end; O1
Row 26: U1; O1; (U2; O2) Repeat to end; U1
Row 27: (O2; U2) Repeat to end; U1
Row 28: O1; U1 (O2; U2) Repeat to end; O1
Row 29: (U2; O2) Repeat to end; O1
Row 30: U1; O1; (U2; O2) Repeat to end; U1
Row 31: O2; (U2; O2) Repeat to end; U1

WEAVING PATTERNS

Although most of the Swatch Critters shown in this book are made using plain-weave squares, there are ways to weave float patterns in squares that would make lovely additions to your Critters! Here are three different weaving patterns for your consideration. You can also create your own float patterns!

Note the following about the abbreviations:

W = Weave Over / Under for the number of threads noted. For example: W7 means to Weave Over / Under 7 threads.

Weave across: Weave across the threads on the loom in normal Over / Under sequence.

U = The tip of your needle goes under a number of threads. For example: U3 means the needle goes Under 3 threads.

O = The tip of your needle goes over a number of threads. For example: O3 means the needle goes Over 3 threads.

Abbreviations within parenthesis mean to treat the instructions in parenthesis as a unit repeated a specified number of times. For example: "(U3; O1) 3 times" means your needle goes Under 3 threads, then Over 1 thread, for 3 repeats in a row.

NOTE: Your needle will always enter going over a loop around the pins. The loop does *not* count for the number of threads involved in the pickup patterns. Example: If the pattern starts U3, the needle enters by going over the loop and then going under the next 3 threads.

Diagonal lines: When joined, the pattern is diagonal lines across the fabric. I think these could be really fun for Ovando the Octopus legs.

Row 1: Weave across
Row 2: U3; W7; U3; W7; U3; W8
Row 3: W6; U3; W7; U3; W7; U3; W2
Row 4: W4; U3; W7; U3; W7; U3; W4
Row 5: W2; U3; W7; U3; W7; U3; W6
Row 6: W8; U3; W7; U3; W7; U3
Row 7: W8; U3; W7; U3; W7; U3 (same as Row 6)
Row 8: W2; U3; W7; U3; W7; U3; W6 (same as Row 5)
Row 9: W4; U3; W7; U3; W7; U3; W4 (same as Row 4)
Row 10: W6; U3; W7; U3; W7; U3; W2 (same as Row 3)
Row 11: U3; W7; U3; W7; U3; W8 (same as Row 2)
Row 12: U3; W7; U3; W7; U3; W8 (same as Row 2)
Row 13: W6; U3; W7; U3; W7; U3; W2 (same as Row 3)
Row 14: W4; U3; W7; U3; W7; U3; W4 (same as Row 4)
Row 15: W2; U3; W7; U3; W7; U3; W6 (same as Row 5)
Row 16: Weave across

APPENDIX

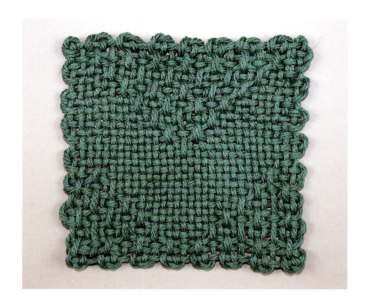

Hourglass: When you seam the squares together, the float triangles and the plain-weave triangles join into diamond shapes. These would be smashing as the squares for Twodot the Turtle's back squares.

Row 1: Weave across

Row 2: W2; (U3, O1) 6 times; U3; W2

Row 3: W4; (U3, O1) 5 times; U3; W4

Row 4: W6; (U3, O1) 4 times; U3; W6

Row 5: W8; (U3, O1) 3 times; U3; W8

Row 6: W10; (U3, O1) 2 times; U3; W10

Row 7: W12; U3; O1; U3; W12

Row 8: W14; U3; W14

Row 9: W14; U3; W14 (same as Row 8)

Row 10: W12; U3; O1; U3; W12 (same as Row 7)

Row 11: W10; (U3, O1) 2 times; U3; W10 (same as Row 6)

Row 12: W8; (U3; O1) 3 times; U3; W8 (same as Row 5)

Row 13: W6; (U3, O1) 4 times; U3; W6 (same as Row 4)

Row 14: W4; (U3, O1) 5 times; U3; W4 (same as Row 3)

Row 15: W2; (U3, O1) 6 times; U3; W2 (same as Row 2)

Row 16: Weave across

Zigzag: When the squares are sewn together, you get a lovely zigzag pattern across and down the fabric. Could be pretty fun for the body squares of Polaris the Penguin to jazz up the "tuxedo look"!

Row 1: Weave across

Row 2: W2; (U3, O1) 6 times; U3; W2

Row 3: W4; (U3, O1) 5 times; U3; W4

Row 4: W6; (U3, O1) 4 times; U3; W6

Row 5: W8; (U3, O1) 3 times; U3; W8

Row 6: W10; (U3, O1) 2 times; U3; W10

Row 7: W12; U3; O1; U3; W12

Row 8: W14; U3; W14

Row 9: Weave across

Row 10: W2; U3; W21; U3; W2

Row 11: U3; O1; U3; W17; U3; O1; U3

Row 12: W2; U3; O1; U3; W13; U3; O1; U3; W2

Row 13: (U3,O1) 2 times; U3; W9; (U3,O1) 2 times; U3

Row 14: W2; (U3; O1) 2 times; U3; W5; (U3; O1) 2 times; U3; W2

Row 15: (U3; O1) 7 times; U3

Row 16: Weave across

167

Acknowledgments

CREATING A BOOK is not a solitary endeavor, and there are many people who made it possible to get this book into your hands. However, there are a few people I need to give a special shout-out to:

Marty Essen, my awesome husband, who was my sounding board and gave valuable critiques when I was designing the original Swatch Critter kits. He also patiently photographed the many, many process photos for the book, sometimes with literally 30 seconds' notice. His patience, support, and photography talents are so greatly appreciated.

Diana McKay and Leslie Taylor, retired owners of Mountain Colors Yarns, were huge supporters of the Swatch Critter kits. Shelby and Sidney the Sheep exist because Diana told me, in no uncertain terms, that I had to create a sheep kit. I can't begin to count the number of times Diana and Leslie would squeeze me into their dyeing schedule to help me meet Swatch Critter kit shipment deadlines or would dye a discontinued colorway for use in the kits. And Diana wrote the knitted sweater pattern for Teton the Teddy. Their help and support over the years is so appreciated.

Sandra Korinchak was my developmental editor at Schiffer Craft Publishing and the first believer in publishing a Swatch Critters pattern book. She kept me on the straight path to completion, which is no small feat!

About the Author

DEB ESSEN lives, weaves, and runs her business, dje handwovens, in the Bitterroot Valley, nestled in the Rocky Mountains of western Montana. She has achieved the Certificate of Excellence in handweaving Level 1 through the handweaver's Guild of America and has been inducted into the Montana Circle of American Masters in Folk and Traditional Art. She has written feature articles for *handwoven* and *Little Looms* magazines. She is also the author of *Easy Weaving with Supplemental Warps: Overshot, Velvet, Shibori, and More*. Her passion is teaching the wonders of weaving, and sharing her knowledge at guilds, regional and national conferences, and other fiber art gatherings. www.djehandwovens.com